SCOTT FORESMAN · ADDISON WESLEY

Mathematics

Grade 4

Practice
Masters/Workbook

PEARSON

Scott
Foresman

Editorial Offices: Glenview, Illinois • Parsippany, New Jersey • New York, New York

Sales Offices: Parsippany, New Jersey • Duluth, Georgia • Glenview, Illinois
Coppell, Texas • Ontario, California • Mesa, Arizona

Overview

Practice Masters provide additional practice on the concept or concepts taught in each lesson.

ISBN 0-328-04956-5

6 7 8 9 10 V084 09 08 07 06 05

Name_____

Numbers in the Thousands

Write each number in standard form.

1.    _____

2. 8 ten thousands + 4 thousands +
   9 hundreds + 4 tens + 7 ones   _____

Write the word form and tell the value of the underlined digit for each number.

3. 7<u>6</u>,239   _____

   _____

4. 823,<u>7</u>74   _____

   _____

5. **Number Sense** Write the number that has 652 in
   the ones period and 739 in the thousands period.   _____

During a weekend at the Movie Palace Theaters, 24,875 tickets were sold. Add the following to the number of tickets sold.

6. 100 tickets _____   7. 1,000 tickets _____

Test Prep

8. Which of the following numbers has a 5 in the
   ten-thousands place?

   A. 652,341   **B.** 562,341   **C.** 462,541   **D.** 265,401

9. **Writing in Math** Explain how you know the 6 in the
   number 364,021 is not in the thousands place.

   _____

   _____

Understanding Greater Numbers

Write the number in standard form and in word form.

1. 300,000,000 + 70,000,000 + 2,000,000 + 500,000 + 10,000 + 2,000 + 800 + 5

_____

_____

Write the word form and tell the value of the underlined digit for each number.

2. 4,600,028 _____

_____

3. 488,423,046 _____

_____

4. **Number Sense** Write the number that is one hundred million more than 15,146,481. _____

5. The population in California in 2000 was 33,871,648. Write the word form.

_____

_____

Test Prep

6. Which is the expanded form for 43,287,005?

   A. 4,000,000 + 300,000 + 20,000 + 8,000 + 700 + 5

   B. 40,000,000 + 3,000,000 + 200,000 + 80,000 + 7,000 + 5

   C. 400,000,000 + 30,000,000 + 2,000,000 + 8,000 + 500

   D. 4,000,000 + 30,000 + 2,000 + 800 + 70 + 5

7. **Writing in Math** In the number 463,211,889, which digit has the greatest value? Explain.

_____

Place-Value Patterns

Name each number in two different ways.

1. 300 _____

_____

2. 2,400 _____

_____

3. 67,000 _____

_____

Reasoning Carlos has 1,300 stamps in his stamp collection.
He is planning on putting his collection into stamp books.
How many pages will he have filled if he puts

4. 10 stamps on each page? _____

5. 100 stamps on each page? _____

Look for a pattern. Find the next three numbers.

6. 4,017 4,027 4,037 _____ _____ _____

7. 11,213 11,313 11,413 _____ _____ _____

Test Prep

8. Which are the next three numbers in the pattern?
2,071 2,141 2,211

A. 2,021 2,041 2,061   **B.** 2,261 2,311 2,361

C. 2,281 2,351 2,421   **D.** 2,311 2,411 2,511

9. Writing in Math Describe the place-value blocks you
could use to show 1,415.

_____

_____

PROBLEM-SOLVING SKILL

Read and Understand

A zoo has 9 cows, 3 horses, 15 chickens, and
12 goats. How many animals are there in all?

1. Tell the problem in your own words.

_____

_____

2. Identify key facts and details.

_____

_____

3. Tell what the question is asking.

_____

_____

4. Show the main idea.

_____

5. Solve the problem. Write the answer in a complete sentence.

_____

For 6 and 7, use the chart below.

6. How many more books does Elaine need
to have the same amount as Juan?

Name	Number of Books
Charlotte	7
Elaine	4
Juan	9

_____

7. How many books do Elaine, Charlotte,
and Juan have altogether?

_____

Comparing and Ordering Numbers

Compare. Write > or < for each ◯ .

1. 2,854,376 ◯ 2,845,763   **2.** 6,789 ◯ 9,876

3. 59,635 ◯ 59,536   **4.** 29,374,125 ◯ 30,743,225

Order the numbers from least to greatest.

5. 45,859,211   4,936,211   43,958,211

_____ _____ _____

6. Number Sense Write three numbers that are greater than 1,543,000 and less than 1,544,000.

_____ _____ _____

7. Put the planets in order from the one closest to the sun to the one farthest from the sun.

_____

_____

_____

_____

The Five Closest Planets to the Sun

Planet	Distance (miles)
Earth	93,000,000
Jupiter	483,000,000
Mars	142,000,000
Mercury	36,000,000
Venus	67,000,000

Test Prep

8. Which number has the greatest value?

A. 86,543,712   **B.** 82,691,111   **C.** 85,381,211   **D.** 86,239,121

9. Writing in Math Tell how you could use a number line to determine which of two numbers is greater.

_____

_____

Name_____

Rounding Numbers

Round each number to the nearest thousand and ten thousand.

1. 68,354   _____   _____

2. 857,836   _____   _____

3. 6,172,438   _____   _____

Round each number to the nearest hundred thousand.

4. 782,954   _____

5. 5,416,755 _____

6. Round the height of Mount Cameroon to the nearest thousand.

_____

7. Round the height of Mount Kilimanjaro to the nearest ten thousand.

_____

African Mountains

Mountain	Height (in feet)
Mount Kilimanjaro	19,340
Mount Cameroon	13,435
Mount Kenya	17,058
Mount Meru	14,979

Test Prep

8. Which is 346,759 rounded to the nearest ten thousand?

A. 300,000   **B.** 346,000   **C.** 350,000   **D.** 400,000

9. Writing in Math Explain how you would round 265,588 to the nearest ten thousand.

_____

_____

_____

The Size of Numbers

One freezer can hold 100 frozen yogurt bars. How many frozen yogurt bars are in

1. 10 freezers? _____   2. 3 freezers? _____

3. 60 freezers? _____   4. 100 freezers? _____

5. How many hundreds equal 1,000? _____

6. How many thousands equal 100,000? _____

7. If on average a tree drops 35 leaves a day in autumn, how many leaves would fall in 10 days? _____

8. If you took a bite of a watermelon and found 8 seeds, about how many seeds would you find in 10 bites?

_____

9. If there are 100 raisins in a box and you have 9 boxes, how many raisins do you have in all?

_____

Test Prep

10. Which of the following is equal to 1,000,000?

   A. 10 boxes with 1,000 trading cards in each box

   B. 100 boxes with 1,000 trading cards in each box

   C. 10 boxes with 10,000 trading cards in each box

   D. 100 boxes with 10,000 trading cards in each box

11. **Writing in Math** How can making small groups help you estimate large numbers?

_____

_____

_____

Name_____

Plan and Solve

Rabbits At Juan's pet shop, the rabbit pen has 25 rabbits in it. Twelve of the rabbits are brown, 2 are black, and 4 are white. The rest are multi-colored. How many multi-colored rabbits are in the pen?

Juan's Work

25			
12	4	2	?

$25 - (12 + 4 + 2) = 7$

1. Name the strategy Juan used to solve the problem.

   _____

2. Give the answer to the problem in a complete sentence.

   _____

   _____

Frozen Yogurt Barbara sells frozen yogurt in cups or cones. The flavors are chocolate, vanilla, caramel, or strawberry. How many different ways can a customer buy frozen yogurt using one flavor and one way to serve it?

		Barbara
Cup		**Cone**
chocolate		chocolate
vanilla		vanilla
caramel		caramel
strawberry		strawberry
8 different ways		

3. Name the strategy Barbara used to solve the problem.

   _____

   _____

4. Give the answer to the problem in a complete sentence.

   _____

   _____

5. What other strategy might Barbara have used?

   _____

Using Money to Understand Decimals

1. 2.18 = _____ ones + _____ tenths + _____ hundredths

   $2.18 = _____ dollars + _____ dimes + _____ pennies

2. 9.27 = _____ ones + _____ hundredths

   $9.27 = _____ dollars + _____ pennies

3. 7.39 = _____ ones + _____ tenths + _____ hundredths

   $7.39 = _____ dollars + _____ dimes + _____ pennies

4. **Number Sense** Write 3 dollars, 9 dimes, and 5 pennies with a dollar sign and decimal point.

   _____

5. **Number Sense** If you have 5 tenths of a dollar, how much money do you have?

   _____

6. Lana wants to buy a book for $6.95. How can she pay for the book using only dollars, dimes, and nickels?

   _____

Test Prep

7. How would you write sixteen and twenty-five hundredths with a decimal point?

   A. 16.025   **B.** 16.25   **C.** 162.5   **D.** 1,625

8. **Writing in Math** Which is greater, 4 tenths and 2 hundredths or 2 tenths and 4 hundredths? Explain.

   _____

   _____

Counting Money

Count the money. Write each amount with a dollar sign and a decimal point.

1. 3 dollars, 5 dimes, 9 pennies = _____

2. 2 five-dollar bills, 3 dollars, 4 dimes = _____

3. 6 dollars, 4 dimes, 7 pennies = _____

4. **Number Sense** Larry has 3 dollars, 7 quarters, and 10 nickels. Can he buy a magazine that costs $5.00? _____

Tell how to make each amount with the fewest bills and coins.

5. $4.26 _____

   _____

6. $6.50 _____

7. $10.31 _____

   _____

8. $35.40 _____

   _____

Test Prep

9. How much money does Lorraine have if she has three $5 bills and 5 quarters?

   A. $3.50   **B.** $13.50   **C.** $15.25   **D.** $16.25

10. **Writing in Math** List the different ways you can make $0.25 without using pennies.

_____

_____

Name_____

Making Change

Tell how you would give change from a $20.00 bill for each purchase. List the bills and coins you would use, and give the amount with a dollar sign and decimal point.

1. $13.55 _____

_____

2. $8.30 _____

_____

Tell how much change you should get from $10.00 when you buy the

$4.79 $6.28 $7.44 $8.33

3. art book. _____   **4.** crafts book. _____

5. music book. _____   **6.** sports book. _____

7. Number Sense Suppose you have $10. Do you have enough money to buy the music book and the art book? Explain.

_____

Test Prep

8. Which of the following is the change you would get when you buy an item that costs $1.29 with two $1 bills?

A. $0.72   **B.** $0.71   **C.** $0.69   **D.** $0.61

9. Writing in Math Imagine that you work in a record store. A customer gives you a $20.00 bill for a CD that costs $15.95. How much change will you give the customer? Explain.

_____

_____

_____

More About Decimals

Write the word form and decimal for each shaded part.

1. _____

2. _____

For each fact, shade a grid to show the part of the population of each country that lives in cities.

3. In Jamaica, 0.5 of the people live in cities.

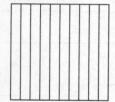

4. Only 0.11 of the population of Uganda live in cities.

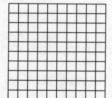

5. In Norway, 0.72 of the people live in cities.

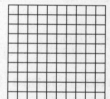

Test Prep

6. Which grid shows fourteen hundredths?

A.   **B.**   **C.**   **D.**

7. Writing in Math Explain why one column in a hundredths grid is equal to one column in a tenths grid.

_____

_____

_____

Name_____

Look Back and Check

Waterfalls Four famous waterfalls
have different heights. Ruacana Falls in
Angola is 406 ft high, Victoria Falls
in Zambia is 343 ft high, Wentworth Falls
in Australia is 614 ft high, and Akaka
Falls in Hawaii is 442 ft high. What is
the order of these waterfalls from the
least to the greatest height?

	William
Waterfalls	Height
Wentworth Falls	614
Akaka Falls	442
Ruacana Falls	406
Victoria Falls	343

The order of the waterfalls
is Wentworth Falls, Akaka
Falls, Ruacana Falls, and
Victoria Falls.

1. Did William answer the right question?

_____

_____

_____

2. Did William's work match the information in the problem?

_____

_____

3. Did William use a correct procedure?

_____

_____

_____

4. Is William's answer reasonable?

_____

_____

_____

Name_____

In Attendance

In 2001, four baseball teams had the following home attendance totals for the season.

2,811,040   3,209,496   2,779,465   3,182,523

1. Write 3,209,496 in expanded form.

   _____

2. Round each attendance total to the nearest hundred thousand.

   _____

   _____

3. Estimate the sum of all four attendance totals.

   _____

4. **Writing in Math** Which estimate gives you more detailed information, rounding to millions or hundred thousands? Explain.

   _____

   _____

   _____

5. Write the attendance totals in order from least to greatest.

   _____

   _____

6. Suppose in one month during 2001, 0.16 of the total season attendance occurred for one team. Show 16 hundredths on the grid by shading the correct number of hundredths.

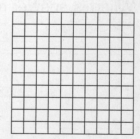

Mental Math: Adding

Add. Use mental math.

1. 89 + 46

_____

2. 301 + 61

_____

3. 400 + 157

_____

4. 722 + 158

_____

5. 523 + 223

_____

6. 804 + 396

_____

7. 299 + 206

_____

8. 878 + 534

_____

9. 1,000 + 7,000

_____

10. Reasoning How can you write
52 + (8 + 25) to make it easier to add?

_____

Use mental math to find the cost of a pound of

11. apples and a pound of oranges.

_____

12. bananas and a pound of grapefruits.

_____

Fruit	Price per Pound
Apple	$0.67
Orange	$0.98
Banana	$0.45
Grapefruit	$0.82

Test Prep

13. Stanley has $10.00. He buys bread for $3.47 and orange
juice for $2.53. How much money does Stanley have left?

A. $3.00   **B.** $4.00   **C.** $6.53   **D.** $8.47

14. Writing in Math Explain how you could add 678 + 303
using mental math.

_____

_____

_____

Mental Math: Subtracting

Subtract. Use mental math.

1. $53 - 21 = $ _____

2. $101 - 49 = $ _____

3. $224 - 26 = $ _____

4. $568 - 352 = $ _____

5. $120 - 33 = $ _____

6. $900 - 187 = $ _____

7. $141 - 98 = $ _____

8. $409 - 11 = $ _____

9. $554 - 59 = $ _____

10. **Number Sense** To subtract 37 from 462 using mental math, you first subtract 40 from 462 and get 422. What should you do next to get the final answer?

_____

Use mental math to find the difference in height between

11. Angel and Tugela.

_____

12. Yosemite and Cuquenan.

_____

World-Class Waterfalls

Name	Height (meters)
Angel	979
Tugela	948
Yosemite	739
Cuquenan	610

Test Prep

13. Dana has 205 cm of ribbon. She uses 64 cm of ribbon to tie a package. Which simpler problems could she use to find out how much ribbon she has left?

   A. $205 - 60$ and $145 - 4$

   B. $205 + 64$ and $269 + 1$

   C. $205 - 60$ and $145 + 4$

   D. $200 - 64$ and $136 - 5$

14. **Writing in Math** Explain how you would count on to find $350 - 156$.

_____

_____

_____

Estimating Sums and Differences

Estimate each sum or difference.

1. 627
    + 95

2. 829
    − 292

3. 987
    − 233

4. 1,568
    + 352

5. 4,263 − 1,613 _____

6. 7,502 + 2,187 _____

7. 24,141 − 2,177 _____

8. 64,099 − 55,555 _____

9. 83,595 + 18,999 _____

10. About how much larger
    is the largest ocean than
    the smallest ocean?

    _____

    _____

    _____

Ocean Area

Ocean	Area (million sq km)
Arctic Ocean	13,986
Atlantic Ocean	82,217
Indian Ocean	73,481
Pacific Ocean	165,384

11. About how many million square kilometers do all the
    oceans together cover?

    _____

Test Prep

12. Mallory is a pilot. Last week she flew the following round trips
    in miles: 2,020; 1,358; 952; 2,258; and 1,888. Which of the
    following is a good estimate of the miles Mallory flew last week?

    A. 6,000 mi   **B.** 6,800 mi   **C.** 7,600 mi   **D.** 8,600 mi

13. **Writing in Math** Explain how you would use front-end
    estimation to subtract 189 from 643.

    _____

    _____

Name_____

Overestimates and Underestimates

Estimate each sum or difference. Then, if possible, tell whether
your estimate is an overestimate or an underestimate.

1. 448 + 492 _____

2. 7,926 − 4,002 _____

3. 1,922 + 4,498 _____

4. 5,647 − 2,089 _____

5. 829 − 673 _____

6. 7,122 + 2,692 _____

7. **Number Sense** Erin estimated 212 + 756
   by adding 200 + 800. Is Erin's estimate an
   overestimate or an underestimate? _____

8. Joel needs $285 for a video game system. He earned $95
   mowing lawns and $112 delivering newspapers. About
   how much more money does Joel need? Explain how you
   estimated. Then tell whether your estimate is an
   overestimate or an underestimate.

   _____

   _____

   _____

Test Prep

9. Which of the following is an estimate of the difference: 3,492 − 1,429?

   A. 700   **B.** 2,000   **C.** 5,000   **D.** 9,000

10. **Writing in Math** Jeremy estimated 927 + 346 by adding 900 + 300.
    Explain why Jeremy's estimate is an underestimate.

    _____

Name_____

Adding Whole Numbers and Money

1. 474
    + 92

2. 947
    + 261

3. 9,746
    + 4,329

4. 2,868
    + 643

5. 87,643
    + 3,892

6. 17,246
    + 42,369

7. $46.96
    + 2.43

8. $45.19
    + 39.46

9. 714 + 395

10. 2,002 + 3,003

11. $8.27 + $29.46

_____

_____

_____

12. **Number Sense** Jacob adds 4,296 and 7,127. Should his answer be greater than or less than 11,000?

_____

Zachary and Travis went out for lunch.

13. Zachary ordered a veggieburger and a large juice. How much was Zachary's total?

Menu	
Veggie burger	$2.75
Fish sandwich	$1.95
Milk	$0.95
Large juice	$2.25

_____

14. Travis ordered a fish sandwich and a milk. How much was his total?

_____

Test Prep

15. Lydia bought a baseball for $6.89 and a baseball bat for $23.46. How much did she spend altogether?

    A. $25.30   **B.** $28.93   **C.** $30.35   **D.** $31.41

16. **Writing in Math** Samuel has 1,482 baseball cards in his collection. Maria gave Samuel 126 cards. How many cards does he have now? Explain what computation method you used and why.

_____

_____

Column Addition

Add.

1.	486 875 + 45	**2.**	$43.34 49.48 + 8.90	**3.**	938 1,487 + 8,947	**4.**	7,226 1,587 + 72,984
5.	$542.36 2.23 + 78.56	**6.**	80 960 4 + 1,986	**7.**	$279.87 20.96 150.98 + 79.45	**8.**	8,738 5,234 836 + 237

9. **Number Sense** Luke added 429 + 699 + 314 and got 950. Is this sum reasonable?

10. What is the combined length of the three longest glaciers?

11. What is the total combined length of the four longest glaciers in the world?

World's Longest Glaciers

Glaciers	Length (miles)
Lambert-Fisher Ice Passage	320
Novaya Zemlya	260
Arctic Institute Ice Passage	225
Nimrod-Lennox-King	180

Test Prep

12. Which is the sum of 3,774 + 8,276 + 102?

A. 1,251 **B.** 12,152 **C.** 13,052 **D.** 102,152

13. **Writing in Math** Leona added 6,641 + 1,482 + 9,879. Should her answer be more than or less than 15,000?

Subtracting Whole Numbers and Money

Subtract.

1. 906
    − 45

2. 3,091
    − 1,361

3. 4,000
    − 2,557

4. 7,242
    − 158

5. $5.23
    − 2.03

6. 8,904
    − 3,596

7. $30.04
    − 21.06

8. 848
    − 257

9. $74.03 − $32.54

10. 5,067 − 2,987

11. $67.97 − $12.98

12. Robert set a goal to swim 1,000 laps in the local swimming pool during his summer break. Robert has currently finished 642 laps. How many more laps does he have to swim in order to meet his goal?

_____

Test Prep

13. Which of the following shows 22 dollars and 7 pennies subtracted from 130 dollars and 10 pennies?

    A. $152.17   **B.** $108.03   **C.** $107.31   **D.** $78.03

14. **Writing in Math** If 694 − 72 = _____, then 622 + _____ = 694. Explain the process of checking your work.

_____

_____

_____

_____

Choose a Computation Method

Add or subtract. Tell what method you used.

1. $5,749
    + 8,274

2. 84,936
    − 27,946

3. 70,000
    + 30,000

4. 56,935
    + 3,964

5. $95,629
    − 7,846

6. 26,000
    − 4,000

7. $3,210 − $1,989 = _____

8. 4,440 + 560 = _____

9. An African elephant weighs 11,023 lb. An
   Asian elephant weighs 8,818 lb. What is
   the total combined weight of an African
   elephant and an Asian elephant?   _____

10. A hippopotamus weighs 4,409 lb.
    A white rhinoceros weighs 4,850 lb.
    How much less does the hippopotamus
    weigh than the white rhinoceros?   _____

Test Prep

11. Which number sentence is easiest to compute using
    mental math?

    A. 1,502 − 685   **B.** 1,530 + 120   **C.** 652 + 989   **D.** 1,596 + 3,628

12. **Writing in Math** Explain how you would use mental math
    to find 1,201 + 8,793. Solve.

    _____

    _____

    _____

Name_____

Look for a Pattern

Look for a pattern. Draw the next two shapes.

1.

2.

Look for a pattern. Write the missing numbers.

3. 5, 8, 11, 14, 17, _____, _____   **4.** 4, 6, 10, 16, 24, _____, _____

Look for a pattern. Complete each number sentence.

5. 80 + 8 = 88

808 + 80 = 888

8,008 + 880 = _____

80,808 + 8,080 = _____

6. 10 + 1 = 11

100 + 1 = 101

1,000 + 1 = _____

10,000 + 1 = _____

Look for a pattern. Write the missing numbers.

7. Sally went to purchase tiles for her kitchen floor. She measured the floor to find how many tiles she needed to cover the floor. Sally decided to make a pattern. She chose 10 red tiles,

20 beige tiles, 30 white tiles, _____ black tiles, and _____ gray tiles to complete a pattern for the kitchen floor.

8. Reasoning Fill in the missing amounts to update Carl's savings passbook.

Carl's Savings Account

Date	Deposit	Balance
4/7	$25	$945
4/14		$995
4/21	$25	
4/30	$50	
5/7		$1,095

Name_____

Translating Words to Expressions

Write a number expression for each phrase.

1. 1,285 is how much more than 622?   _____

2. $402 increased by $86   _____

3. 946 beads, then 80 fewer beads   _____

4. 12 adults combined with 26 children   _____

Write a number expression and then solve.

5. How many people do the 8 in. salad bowl and the 12 in. salad bowl serve together?

   _____

Cathy's Salads

Size	Servings	Price
8 in. bowl	4	$12.00
10 in. bowl	6	$15.00
12 in. bowl	8	$18.00

6. How much more money does the 12 in. salad bowl cost compared to the 10 in. one?

   _____

Write a number expression for the situation.

7. The bicycle museum had 220 fewer visitors this month than last month, when 980 people visited. How many people visited the museum this month?

   _____

8. **Writing in Math** Write a word problem that can be solved using the expression 96 − 23.

   _____

   _____

   _____

Matching Words and Number Expressions

Choose the number expression that matches the words. Then, find its value.

1. Jaleesa made 24 blueberry muffins. She gave 10 muffins to her friends. Then Jaleesa made 2 more muffins.

   $24 - (10 + 2)$ or $(24 - 10) + 2$

   _____

2. Antoine brought 24 bottles of juice to the picnic. The 14 people at the picnic each had 1 juice with their lunch. After the kids played soccer, Antoine's dad arrived with 12 more bottles of juice.

   $(24 - 14) + 12$ or $24 - (14 + 12)$

   _____

Choose the number expression that matches the words. Then, find its value.

3. Saturn has 18 moons, Jupiter has 16 moons, and Neptune has 8 moons. How many more moons do Saturn and Jupiter have combined than Neptune?

   $(18 + 16) - 8$ or $18 + (16 - 8)$

   _____

Test Prep

4. Which of the following is the value of the number expression $50 - (17 + 18)$?

   A. 25   **B.** 20   **C.** 15   **D.** 10

5. **Writing in Math** Explain which operation you would do first in the expression $47 - (17 + 12)$.

   _____

   _____

Name _____

Evaluating Expressions

Evaluate each expression for $y = 15$.

1. $y + 15$ _____

2. $y + 39$ _____

3. $85 - y$ _____

4. $51 - y$ _____

Find the missing numbers in each table.

5.

n	$n + 35$
2	
10	45
15	
95	

6.

x	$75 - x$
9	
25	50
35	
52	

7. Kiara saved $27. She bought her mother a gift. She has $13 left. How much did she spend on the gift? _____

8. Carlos had 11 cans of paint. He used 4 cans painting the garage. He bought 2 more cans. How many cans of paint does Carlos have now? _____

Test Prep

9. Which is the value of $a + 235$ when $a = 150$?

A. 85   **B.** 150   **C.** 385   **D.** 485

10. Writing in Math Explain how to evaluate $44 + x$ for $x = 34$.

_____

_____

Solving Addition and Subtraction Equations

Solve each equation.

1. $d - 12 = 12$ $d =$ _____

2. $82 + b = 90$ $b =$ _____

3. $f + 50 = 300$ $f =$ _____

4. $q - 800 = 200$ $q =$ _____

5. $9 + k = 18$ $k =$ _____

6. $90 - w = 88$ $w =$ _____

7. **Number Sense** Is the solution of $25 + n = 30$ greater or less than 30? Explain how you know without solving.

_____

_____

8. Andre bought a model airplane. He also bought a tube of glue for $6. He spent $22. Use the equation $a + \$6 = \$22$ to find the cost of the model airplane. _____

Test Prep

9. Which is the value of the variable in the equation $r - 126 = 19$?

   A. 245   **B.** 145   **C.** 107   **D.** 49

10. **Writing in Math** Explain how the variable b has two different values in the two equations.

   $6 - b = 5$ $b = 1$ $b + 5 = 15$ $b = 10$

_____

_____

_____

Name_____

A Piece of History

The Statue of Liberty, located on Liberty Island in New York, was given to the United States as a present from France on July 4, 1884. The statue was still in France at the time. It was taken apart and then shipped in sections to the United States in 1885.

A total of 350 pieces of the statue were shipped on the French transport ship *Isere*. The pieces were shipped in a total of 214 crates.

1. Suppose that, after arriving in the United States, it took two days to remove the first 108 crates. How many crates were still on the ship?

   _____

2. Suppose four different pieces of the statue had the following weights: 4,219 lb; 3,182 lb; 876 lb; and 1,215 lb. Find the total weight of the four pieces.

   _____

3. Admission to the Statue of Liberty is free. In 2002, the price for three adults to ride the ferry round trip was $21. The price for five adults was $35. What is the round-trip price for one adult?

   _____

4. Suppose there are 13 children who take the ferry during one trip to the Statue of Liberty. A total of 51 people take the trip. Write a number sentence to find the number of adults who take the ferry. Solve. Write your answer in a complete sentence.

   _____

   _____

   _____

Meanings for Multiplication

Write an addition sentence and a multiplication sentence for the picture.

1.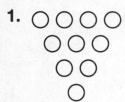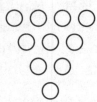

_____

Write a multiplication sentence for each addition sentence.

2. 4 + 4 + 4 + 4 = 16 _____

3. 10 + 10 + 10 + 10 + 10 + 10 = 60 _____

4. Number Sense How could you use multiplication to find 7 + 7 + 7?

_____

5. A classroom desk has 4 legs. How many legs do
5 desks have altogether? _____

6. Danielle planted 3 seeds in 6 different pots.
How many seeds did she plant? _____

Test Prep

7. Which is the multiplication sentence for 2 + 2 + 2 + 2?

   A. 4 × 4 = 16   **B.** 2 × 2 = 4   **C.** 4 × 2 = 8   **D.** 2 × 6 = 12

8. Writing in Math Explain how you can use multiplication to
find 2 + 2 + 2 + 2.

_____

_____

_____

Name_____

Patterns in Multiplying
by 0, 1, 2, 5, and 9

1. $\begin{array}{r} 5 \\ \times\ 4 \\ \hline \end{array}$ 2. $\begin{array}{r} 2 \\ \times\ 3 \\ \hline \end{array}$ 3. $\begin{array}{r} 7 \\ \times\ 1 \\ \hline \end{array}$ 4. $\begin{array}{r} 5 \\ \times\ 0 \\ \hline \end{array}$

5. $\begin{array}{r} 8 \\ \times\ 2 \\ \hline \end{array}$ 6. $\begin{array}{r} 5 \\ \times\ 3 \\ \hline \end{array}$ 7. $\begin{array}{r} 8 \\ \times\ 0 \\ \hline \end{array}$ 8. $\begin{array}{r} 4 \\ \times\ 1 \\ \hline \end{array}$

9. $9 \times 6 =$ _____   10. $7 \times 2 =$ _____   11. $0 \times 0 =$ _____

Algebra Find the missing number. Tell which property can help you.

12. _____ $\times\ 9 = 0$

_____

13. $1 \times$ _____ $= 4$

_____

14. A package of baseball cards includes
    5 cards. How many baseball cards are
    in 5 packages?   _____

Test Prep

15. What is the value of the missing number?
    $\square \times 9 = 36$

    A. 6   **B.** 4   **C.** 3   **D.** 2

16. **Writing in Math** Milton needs to find the product of two
    numbers. One of the numbers is 9. The answer also needs
    to be 9. How will he solve this problem? Explain.

_____

_____

_____

Name_____

Using Known Facts to Find
Unknown Facts

Use breaking apart to find each product.

1. 7
   × 3

2. 9
   × 5

3. 8
   × 2

4. 6
   × 4

5. $4 \times 3 =$ _____

6. $9 \times 3 =$ _____

7. $8 \times 5 =$ _____

8. $3 \times 6 =$ _____

9. $6 \times 7 =$ _____

10. $7 \times 9 =$ _____

11. Number Sense Sara traced circle stencils for her project.
She needs 7 rows of 9 circle stencils. She thought that
7 rows of 9 is the same as 3 rows of 9 and 2 rows of 9.
Is this correct?

_____

_____

_____

Reasoning Compare. Use <, >, or = to fill in each blank ◯ .

12. 6×9 ◯ 9×6

13. 9×4 ◯ 6×6

14. 8×8 ◯ 7×9

Test Prep

15. Which of the following is equal to the product of 3×3?

A. 9×1 **B.** 3×1 **C.** 4×2 **D.** 6×3

16. Writing in Math Explain how the three multiplication
sentences are related.
12×2 8×3 6×4

_____

Multiplying by 10, 11, and 12

1. $4 \times 10 =$ _____   2. $12 \times 2 =$ _____   3. $10 \times 6 =$ _____

4. $11 \times 1 =$ _____   5. $4 \times 12 =$ _____   6. $8 \times 11 =$ _____

7. $9 \times 10 =$ _____   8. $12 \times 3 =$ _____   9. $10 \times 7 =$ _____

10. $11 \times 5 =$ _____   11. $10 \times 5 =$ _____   12. $6 \times 12 =$ _____

13. **Number Sense** Beatrice multiplied 10×9. She quickly found the answer by placing a 0 behind the 9 to get an answer of 90. Is this reasonable?

_____

_____

There are 12 months in 1 year. How many months are in

14. 2 years? _____

15. 3 years? _____

16. 5 years? _____

17. In the classroom there are 5 round tables. There are 4 students sitting at each table. How many students are sitting at the tables altogether? _____

Test Prep

18. How much money is 12 dimes?

   A. $0.60   **B.** $1.00   **C.** $1.20   **D.** $2.00

19. **Writing in Math** Explain how to find 7×11.

_____

_____

Name_____

Make a Table

Complete the table to solve the problem. Write the answer in a
complete sentence.

1. The grocery store is having a sale on canned vegetables.
   If you buy 1 can, you get 2 free. How many cans do you
   need to buy to get 16 cans free?

Cans purchased	1	2	3	4	5	6	7	8	9
Free cans	2	4							

2. Grandma wanted to help Jennifer learn to multiply. On the
   first day of Jennifer's visit, Grandma gave her 2 charms for
   her charm bracelet. On the second day, Grandma gave
   Jennifer 4 charms. On the third day, she gave Jennifer
   8 charms. How many charms did Grandma give Jennifer
   on the sixth day of her visit?

Day	1	2	3	4	5	6	7
Charms	2	4	8				

For Exercise 3, make a table. Use it to find the answer.

3. Juan decided to raise money for his camping trip
   by selling lemonade. He charged $1.00 for 1 glass,
   $1.25 for 2 glasses, $1.50 for 3 glasses, and
   so on. How much money did Juan charge for 5
   glasses of lemonade?   _____

Name_____

Meanings for Division

Draw pictures to solve each problem.

1. There are 12 small gift bags. Each bag can hold 1 toy and some stickers. There are 36 stickers. If an equal number of stickers is put in each bag, how many stickers will be in each bag?

    _____

2. One egg carton holds 12 eggs. How many cartons are you able to fill with 60 eggs?

    _____

3. There are 21 students in Mr. Tentler's class. The students divided themselves evenly into 3 groups. How many students are in each group?   _____

Test Prep

4. Calvin read an 18-page chapter in his social studies book in 2 hours. If he read the same number of pages each hour, how many pages did he read per hour?

    A. 3 pages   **B.** 6 pages   **C.** 9 pages   **D.** 12 pages

5. **Writing in Math** The class is planning a party. The pizza restaurant cuts each pizza into 8 slices. There are 32 students. How many pizzas does the class need to order for each student to have a slice? Explain.

    _____

    _____

Name_____

Relating Multiplication and Division

Complete each fact family.

1. $7 \times$ _____ $= 42$

   _____ $\times$ _____ $= 42$

   $42 \div 6 =$ _____

   $42 \div$ _____ $=$ _____

2. $9 \times$ _____ $= 36$

   _____ $\times$ _____ $= 36$

   $36 \div 4 =$ _____

   $36 \div$ _____ $=$ _____

Write a fact family for each set of numbers.

3. 6, 3, 18

   _____

4. 5, 5, 25

   _____

5. **Reasoning** Why does the fact family for 81 and 9 have only two number sentences?

   _____

   _____

   _____

Test Prep

6. Which number sentence completes the fact family?

   $9 \times 6 = 54$ $54 \div 9 = 6$ $54 \div 6 = 9$

   A. $9 \times 9 = 81$ **B.** $6 \times 9 = 54$ **C.** $6 \times 6 = 36$ **D.** $8 \times 6 = 48$

7. **Writing in Math** Find two ways to divide 16 evenly. Explain.

   _____

   _____

Name_____

Division Facts

1. $9 \div 3 =$ _____   2. $21 \div 7 =$ _____   3. $30 \div 5 =$ _____

4. $56 \div 8 =$ _____   5. $72 \div 9 =$ _____   6. $48 \div 8 =$ _____

7. $9\overline{)81}$ _____   8. $6\overline{)54}$ _____   9. $7\overline{)49}$ _____   10. $3\overline{)27}$ _____

11. **Reasoning** If $44 \div 4 = 11$, what is $44 \div 11$? Explain.

_____

_____

_____

_____

12. Taylor bought a CD for $10. How many CDs can she buy for $40?   _____

13. Christian placed an order with the book club. He purchased 2 books for $3 each and a stamp-making kit that costs $5. What was his total?   _____

Test Prep

14. Which is the quotient of $48 \div 6$?

   A. 8   **B.** 6   **C.** 4   **D.** 9

15. **Writing in Math** If $9 \times 8 = 72$, then 72 divided by 8 is what number? Explain how you know without actually finding the quotient.

_____

_____

_____

_____

Name_____

Special Quotients

1. $0 \div 10 =$ _____   2. $7 \div 1 =$ _____   3. $8 \div 8 =$ _____

4. $9 \div 9 =$ _____   5. $0 \div 5 =$ _____   6. $5 \div 1 =$ _____

7. $1\overline{)4}$ _____   8. $8\overline{)0}$ _____   9. $3\overline{)3}$ _____   10. $1\overline{)6}$ _____

11. **Number Sense** If $x \div 9 = 1$, how do you know what x is? Explain.

_____

_____

12. Kenneth has 22 math problems to do for homework. He
    has 12 problems done. How many more problems does he
    have left? If he completes 1 problem every minute, how
    many more minutes does he have to work?

_____

13. There are 8 people who would like to share a box of
    granola bars that contains 8 bars. How many granola bars
    does each person get if they share equally?

_____

Test Prep

14. Which is the quotient of $20 \div 20$?

    A. 20   **B.** 2   **C.** 1   **D.** 0

15. **Writing in Math** Write a rule for the following number
    sentence: $0 \div 7 = 0$.

_____

_____

_____

Multiplication and Division Stories

Reasoning Write a multiplication or division story for each number fact. Solve.

1. $12 \div 3 =$ _____

_____

2. $4 \times 5 =$ _____

_____

3. $50 \div 10 =$ _____

_____

4. $3 \times 9 =$ _____

_____

Use the data in the table to write a multiplication story for the number fact. Solve.

5. $2 \times 6 =$ _____

_____

_____

First Aid Kit

Supply	Number in Kit
Bandages	4
Cleanser pads	6
Cotton balls	12

Test Prep

6. Which is the quotient of $28 \div 7$?

A. 14   **B.** 9   **C.** 6   **D.** 4

7. Writing in Math Write a division story for 12 and 3.

_____

_____

Multiple-Step Problems

Write and answer the hidden question or questions.
Then solve the problem. Write your answer in a
complete sentence.

County Fair Admission	
Adults	$5.00
Students	$3.00
Children	$2.00

1. Mario and his family went to the county
   fair. They bought 2 adult passes and
   3 children's passes. What was the
   total cost for the family?

   _____

   _____

   _____

2. A bus has 12 rows with 1 seat in each row on one side and
   12 rows with 2 seats in each row on the other side. How
   many seats does the bus have altogether?

   _____

   _____

   _____

3. **Writing in Math** Write a problem about going to the laundromat
   that has a hidden question. A single load of laundry costs $2 and
   a double load costs $4. Solve your problem.

   _____

   _____

   _____

Name_____

Writing and Evaluating Expressions

Evaluate each expression for $b = 6$.

1. $6b = $ _____   **2.** $\frac{42}{b} = $ _____   **3.** $5b = $ _____   **4.** $\frac{b}{3} = $ _____

Evaluate each expression for $c = 4$.

5. $\frac{c}{2} = $ _____   **6.** $12c$ _____   **7.** $8c$ _____   **8.** $\frac{16}{c} = $ _____

Evaluate each expression.

9. $(84 \div z) - 6$ for $z = 7$ _____   **10.** $(48 \div h) \times 2$ for $h = 8$ _____

Draw a picture that shows the main idea. Then write and evaluate an expression to solve the problem.

11. Diedre helps read to the kindergarten class. She is assigned to q students. She reads for 10 min with each student. Write an expression to represent the total number of minutes Diedre reads with kindergarten students. Evaluate the expression for $q = 5$.

_____

_____

Test Prep

12. Solve.
$24 \div n = 12$

A. $n = 5$ **B.** $n = 4$ **C.** $n = 3$ **D.** $n = 2$

13. Writing in Math Keith wrote the expression $10d$ to represent the number of dimes in d dollars. Is Keith's expression correct? Explain.

_____

_____

Name _____

Find a Rule

Complete each table. Write the rule.

1.

In	7	6	5	4	3	n
Out	21	18	15	12		

_____

2.

In	5	10	15	20	25	n
Out	1	2	3	4		

_____

In one week, Lyle read 40 pages in his book and his dad gave him 5 stickers. The next week, Lyle read 16 pages and his dad gave him 2 stickers. The third week, Lyle read 56 pages and his dad gave him 7 stickers.

Pages	40	16	56	
Stickers	5	2	7	4

3. Complete the table to show how many pages Lyle had to read to receive 4 stickers from his dad.

_____

4. Write a rule for the table.

_____

Test Prep

5. What is the rule for the table at the right?

In	2	4	6	8	10
Out	14	28	42	56	70

A. Divide by 7   **B.** Multiply by 7   **C.** Divide by 8   **D.** Multiply by 8

6. Writing in Math Complete the table to represent the pattern in figures. Write a rule.

Figure	1	2	3
Circles			

Figure 1   Figure 2   Figure 3

Solving Multiplication and Division Equations

Solve each equation by testing these values for y: 3, 4, 6, and 12.

1. $5 \times y = 15$ _____

2. $\frac{24}{y} = 4$ _____

Solve each equation by testing these values for a: 7, 8, 77, and 80.

3. $14 \div a = 2$ _____

4. $7 \times 11 = a$ _____

5. John's teacher made 20 First Day of School Kits. There were only 4 kits of each color. Solve the equation $4k = 20$ by testing these values for k: 2, 3, 4, and 5, to find how many different colors John's teacher used for the kits.

Test Prep

6. Which is the solution for $n \div 6 = 8$?

   A. 8　　　　　B. 16　　　　　C. 32　　　　　D. 48

7. **Writing in Math** Draw a picture and write an expression you could use to find the number of magazines in m rows if there are 7 magazines in each row. Use your expression to find the number of magazines in 3 rows.

Name_____

Dr. Seuss's Books

Dr. Seuss was one of America's most famous authors and illustrators of children's books. His real name was Theodore Geisel. Geisel was born in 1904 in Springfield, Massachusetts. Geisel's first job was drawing cartoon advertisements for a company that made bug spray. Many of the cartoon characters Geisel drew for that job turned into the characters he used in his books.

1. Each Dr. Seuss hardcover book costs about $9. How much would you pay if you bought 5 books? _____

2. Oscar found a special sale on Dr. Seuss books. Each book costs the same price. He paid $36 for 6 books. How much did he pay for each book? _____

Mrs. Melvin, a librarian, found a special on-line offer for Dr. Seuss books. Each book costs $2.

3. How much did Mrs. Melvin pay for 6 books? _____

4. If Mrs. Melvin paid $20 for *n* books, how many books did she order? _____

One of Dr. Seuss's most famous books is called *The Foot Book*.

5. There are 27 pages in this book. There are about 27 drawings. On the average, about how many drawings are on each page?

_____

6. A close study of this book shows that on 6 pages the word *feet* appears 2 times. What is the total number of times the word appears on those 6 pages? _____

7. On every 9th page of this book, the word *feet* appears 3 times. Since there are 27 pages in the book, how many pages have the word *feet* written 3 times? _____

Name_____

Telling Time

Write the time shown on each clock in two ways.

1.

_____

_____

2.

_____

_____

3. Jessica has a piano lesson on Saturday
   at 2:00. Is it A.M. or P.M.?   _____

4. **Reasoning** The digits displayed on this clock are all
   the same number. List all of the times when this is true.

   _____

5. **Estimation** The time is 2:57 P.M. About what
   time will it be in an hour and a half?   _____

Test Prep

6. Which time is shown on the clock?

   A. 8:24   **B.** 8:34

   C. 8:44   **D.** 8:54

7. **Writing in Math** List two events that could happen
   in the A.M. and two events that could happen in the P.M.

   _____

   _____

Units of Time

Write >, <, or = for each $\bigcirc$.

1. 48 hours $\bigcirc$ 4 days
2. 1 year $\bigcirc$ 12 months

3. 60 minutes $\bigcirc$ 2 hours
4. 17 days $\bigcirc$ 2 weeks

5. 5 months $\bigcirc$ 40 weeks
6. 1 millennium $\bigcirc$ 10 centuries

7. 6 decades $\bigcirc$ 1 century
8. 5 decades $\bigcirc$ 48 years

9. Cheryl's grandparents have been married for 6 decades. How many years have they been married? _____

10. Tom was in elementary school from 1997 to 2002. How much time was that in years? _____

The Declaration of Independence was signed on July 4, 1776. The United States celebrated the bicentennial on July 4, 1976. How much time was that in

11. years? _____
12. decades? _____

Test Prep

13. 49 days =

   A. 5 weeks   B. 6 weeks   C. 7 weeks   D. 8 weeks

14. **Writing in Math** Which is longer: 180 sec or 3 min? Explain how you decided.

_____

_____

_____

Name_____

Elapsed Time

Find each elapsed time.

1. Start: 3:52 P.M.
Finish: 4:10 P.M.

_____

2. Start: 11:35 A.M.
Finish: 12:25 P.M.

_____

3. Start: 3:15 P.M.
Finish: 5:00 P.M.

_____

4. Start: 8:20 A.M.
Finish: 2:35 P.M.

_____

Write the time each clock will show in 30 min.

5.

_____

6.

_____

7.

_____

8. Number Sense Max says that the elapsed time from 11:55 A.M. to 1:10 P.M. is more than an hour and a half. Is he correct? Explain.

_____

Test Prep

9. Gary began eating lunch at 12:17 P.M. and finished at 1:01 P.M. Which is the elapsed time?

A. 41 min   **B.** 42 min   **C.** 43 min   **D.** 44 min

10. Writing in Math Ella went in the swimming pool at 1:20 P.M. She swam for 1 hr and 20 min. What time was it when she finished swimming?

_____

46   Use with Lesson 4-3.

Name_____

Writing to Compare

1. Write two statements comparing the times on the train schedule.

Train Schedule

Stop	Downtown	A	B	C	D	E	F	G	Uptown
Blue Line	8:00	8:02	8:06	8:10	8:20	8:26	8:32	8:40	8:46
Red Line	8:05	—	8:10	8:14	—	8:28	—	8:38	8:44

_____

_____

_____

Summer Day-Camp Schedule

Group 1	Group 2	Times
First aid	Badminton	9:50–10:20
Swimming	Gardening	10:25–11:00
Computers	Sewing	11:05–11:35
Writing	Swimming	11:40–12:05
Lunch	Lunch	12:10–12:45

2. How long is the first-aid class?   _____

3. How long is the gardening class?   _____

4. How much time do campers have between
   classes?   _____

5. Write two statements comparing the schedules of Group 1 and Group 2.

_____

_____

_____

Name_____

Calendars

Use the October and November calendars for 1–8.

October						
S	M	T	W	T	F	S
				1	2	3
4	5	6	7	8	9	10
11	12	13	14	15	16	17
18	19	20	21	22	23	24
25	26	27	28	29	30	31

November						
S	M	T	W	T	F	S
1	2	3	4	5	6	7
8	9	10	11	12	13	14
15	16	17	18	19	20	21
22	23	24	25	26	27	28
29	30					

Find the date

1. six weeks after October 9th.

_____

2. two weeks before November 24th.

_____

3. one week after October 30th.

_____

4. three weeks after November 1st.

_____

5. Suppose you have guitar lessons every Wednesday. What are the dates of your lessons in October?

_____

6. **Number Sense** Find the date five days after November 30, without a calendar.   _____

Test Prep

7. Which amount of time is greatest?

A. 30 days

B. the number of days in October

C. the number of days in November

D. All of the above are equal.

8. **Writing in Math** Use the October calendar. Explain how you can find the number of days that are between October 8th and October 23rd without counting the days.

_____

_____

Name_____

Pictographs

How many people prefer a

Favorite Books

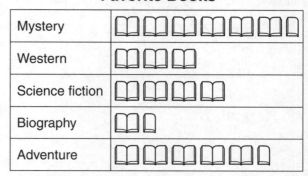

1. western book?

_____

2. mystery book?

_____

3. About how many more people will read an adventure book than a science-fiction book?

_____

4. **Number Sense** Do more than or less than twice as many people prefer science fiction than biography?

_____

5. Make a pictograph of the data about Angela's leaf collection.

Angela's Leaf Collection	
Tamarac	11
Silver birch	7
Oak	5
Maple	10
Sassafras	15

Test Prep

Use the Favorite Books pictograph for 6 and 7.

6. Which type of book was chosen by about 15 people?

   A. Adventure   **B.** Biography   **C.** Mystery   **D.** Science fiction

7. **Writing in Math** Write your own problem for this pictograph. Then solve it.

_____

_____

Name_____

Line Plots

How many soccer teams scored

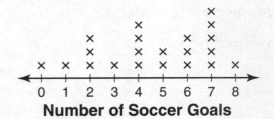

Number of Soccer Goals

1. 5 goals?

_____

2. 2 goals?

_____

3. 3 goals?

_____

4. Number Sense Suppose the line plot was made in the middle of the season. For the teams that have scored 7 goals, how many goals do you predict they will score at the end of the season? _____

5. Make a line plot of the grams of protein in the food listed.

Grams of Protein in One Serving

Food	Grams
Bacon	6
Black beans	15
Cheese pizza	15
Crabmeat	23
Fish stick	6
Great northern beans	14

Test Prep

Use the Soccer League line plot for 6 and 7.

6. How many teams are recorded on the line plot?

A. 18   **B.** 19   **C.** 20   **D.** 21

7. Writing in Math Is there an outlier in the data? Explain.

Bar Graphs

How many free-throw shots did

1. Jan make?

_____

2. Bob make?

_____

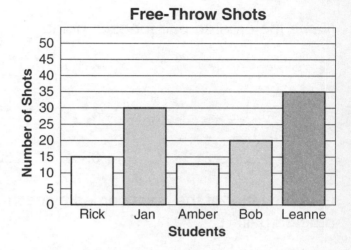

Free-Throw Shots

Who made

3. 35 free-throw shots?

_____

4. 15 free-throw shots?

_____

5. Number Sense How can you easily tell who completed about the same number of free-throw shots?

_____

_____

Test Prep

6. What are the numbers that show the units on a graph called?

A. Scale   **B.** Intervals   **C.** Horizontal axis **D.** Vertical axis

7. Writing in Math Describe the interval you would use for a bar graph if the data ranges from 12 to 39 units.

_____

_____

Graphing Ordered Pairs

Name the ordered pair for each point.

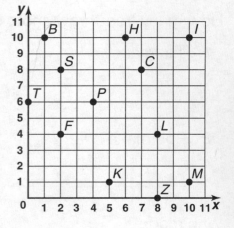

1. P _____

2. H _____

3. L _____

4. F _____

5. K _____

6. Z _____

Give the letter of the point named by each ordered pair.

7. (7, 8) _____

8. (10, 1) _____

9. (2, 8) _____

10. (0, 6) _____

11. (10, 10) _____

12. (1, 10) _____

13. Number Sense How are the coordinates (1, 2) and (3, 2) related?

_____

_____

Test Prep

14. Which letter is named by (9, 3)?

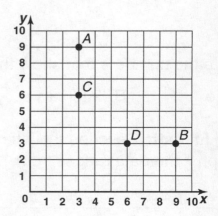

A. A

B. B

C. C

D. D

15. Writing in Math Explain how to plot point G (2, 7) on a coordinate grid.

_____

_____

52 Use with Lesson 4-9.

Name_____

Line Graphs

In the Fourth-Grade Reading Program, how many pages were read in

1. October?

_____

2. February?

_____

3. April?

_____

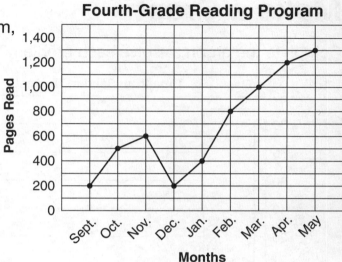

Fourth-Grade Reading Program

4. Draw a line graph showing Barbara's exercise time.

Barbara's Exercise Times

Day	Length of Time
1	25 min
2	30 min
3	40 min

5. Reasoning What is the trend in the data?

_____

_____

Test Prep

6. What is an increase or decrease on a line graph called?

   A. Trend   **B.** Median   **C.** Mode   **D.** Range

7. Writing in Math Explain how a line graph is similar to a bar graph.

_____

Name_____

Make a Graph

Complete the graph to solve each problem.

1.

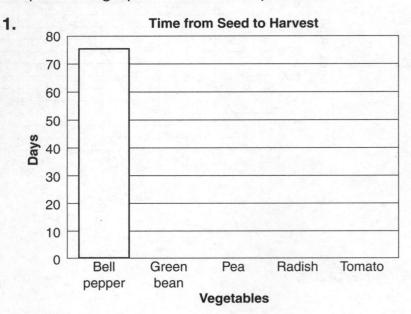

Time from Seed to Harvest

Vegetable	Days
Bell pepper	75
Green bean	56
Pea	75
Radish	23
Tomato	73

2. Which vegetables take the greatest amount of time to harvest? How much greater is this number of days than the number of days needed to harvest radishes?

_____

_____

3. Which vegetable plant will be ready to harvest earlier, the bell pepper plant or the tomato plant? How many days earlier?

_____

4. Number Sense Which vegetable plants will be ready to harvest within 5 days of the tomato plant?

_____

5. Write the missing numbers.   7, 10, 13, 16, _____, _____, _____

Median, Mode, and Range

Find the median, mode, and range of each set of data.

1. 1, 3, 10, 8, 7, 3, 11

_____

2. 48, 50, 62, 50, 54

_____

3. 92, 99, 99, 106, 99, 97

_____

4. 80, 85, 87, 80, 89

_____

5. 10, 11, 12, 14, 10, 15, 16, 10, 11, 9, 10, 17, 10

_____

6. 5, 15, 17, 5, 11, 5, 10, 12, 5, 7, 14, 9, 5

_____

7. Number Sense Could 5 be the mode of 5, 9, 7, 5, 8, 7, 10, and 7? Explain.

_____

_____

Use the bar graph.

8. Find the median, mode, and range of the finished journal entries.

_____

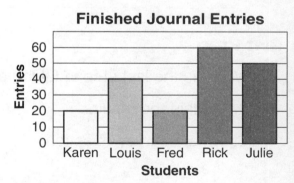

Finished Journal Entries

Test Prep

9. The range of 1, 3, 4, 6, 1, 3, 4, 2, 7, 4, 1, and 4 is

A. 5　　　　**B.** 6　　　　**C.** 7　　　　**D.** 8

10. Writing in Math Tell when a set of data can have no mode.

_____

_____

Name_____

Data from Surveys

Use the data in the tally chart.

Favorite Frozen Yogurt	
Banana	|||
Blueberry	~~||||~~ ~~||||~~ ||
Strawberry	~~||||~~
Vanilla	~~||||~~ |||

1. How many people in the survey liked strawberry-flavored frozen yogurt best?

   _____

2. Which flavor of frozen yogurt received the most votes?

   _____

3. How many people liked vanilla frozen yogurt best?

   _____

4. How many people were surveyed?

   _____

5. **Number Sense** Could the frozen yogurt survey help restaurants choose flavors of frozen yogurt? Explain.

   _____

   _____

   _____

Test Prep

6. Which is the last step in taking a survey?

   A. explain the results

   C. write a survey question

   B. count tallies

   D. make a tally chart and ask the question

7. **Writing in Math** Give an example of a topic for a survey question where the results for the answers could be similar.

   _____

   _____

   _____

56

Misleading Graphs

Use the Price Paid for CD Player bar graph for 1–4.

Price Paid for CD Player

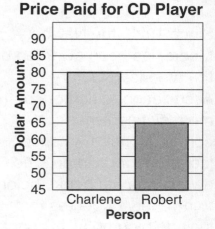

1. Looking at the graph, how much more does it seem Charlene paid compared to Robert?

   _____

2. What was the cost for each CD player?

   _____

   _____

3. Did Charlene pay twice as much as Robert for her player? _____

4. Why is the graph misleading?

   _____

Use the Party Decorations Challenge bar graph for 5–7.

Party Decorations Challenge

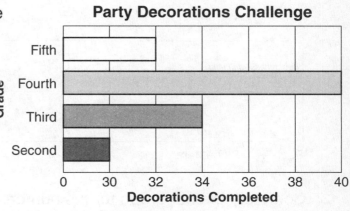

5. Looking at the graph, how many more party decorations does it seem the third grade made compared to the second grade?

   _____

6. Did the fourth grade complete twice the number of party decorations compared to the third grade?

   _____

Test Prep

7. **Writing in Math** Describe a better scale to use for this bar graph.

   _____

   _____

Name_____

The Newbery Medal

Since 1923, the Newbery Medal has been awarded by the American Library Association to authors of the most distinguished contributions to American literature for children. The award-winning books belong to a variety of genres that include biography, historical fiction, and science fiction.

Title and Author	Year	Chapters	Pages
A Year Down Yonder by Richard Peck	2001	8	130
Maniac Magee by Jerry Spinelli	1991	46	184
Jacob Have I Loved by Katherine Patterson	1981	20	215

The table above gives information about three Newbery Medal winners.

1. Complete the pictograph for the number of chapters in the three books.

Chapters in Three Newbery Medal Books

Book	Chapters
A Year Down Yonder	
Maniac Magee	

Each ■ = 2 chapters.

2. Complete the bar graph for the number of pages in each book.

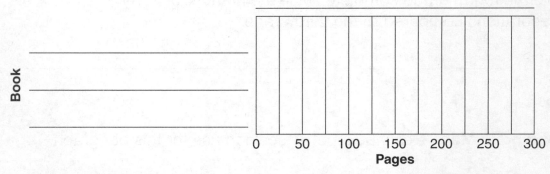

3. Describe the pattern you see between the years the medals were awarded.

_____

Multiplying by Multiples of 10, 100, or 1,000

Find each product. Use mental math.

1. $6 \times 70 =$ _____ **2.** $80 \times 2 =$ _____

3. $40 \times 9 =$ _____ **4.** $10 \times 3 =$ _____

5. $4 \times 500 =$ _____ **6.** $300 \times 9 =$ _____

7. $8 \times 600 =$ _____ **8.** $7 \times 400 =$ _____

9. $6 \times 2,000 =$ _____ **10.** $8,000 \times 5 =$ _____

11. $8 \times 6,000 =$ _____ **12.** $4,000 \times 3 =$ _____

13. **Number Sense** How many zeros will the product of $7 \times 5,000$ have? _____

Mr. Young has 30 times as many pencils as Jack. The whole school has 2,000 times as many pencils as Jack. If Jack has 2 pencils, how many pencils does

14. Mr. Young have? **15.** the whole school have?

_____ _____

Test Prep

16. Find $3 \times 1,000$.

A. 30 **B.** 300 **C.** 3,000 **D.** 30,000

17. **Writing in Math** Wendi says that the product of 5×400 will have 2 zeros. Is she correct? Explain.

_____

_____

_____

Name_____

Estimating Products

Estimate each product.

1. 7×42 is close to $7 \times$ _____

2. 9×511 is close to $9 \times$ _____

3. 5×79 _____

4. 6×32 _____

5. 4×63 _____

6. 8×102 _____

7. 9×354 _____

8. 3×428 _____

9. 7×493 _____

10. 5×814 _____

11. $2 \times 3,541$ _____

12. 8×783 _____

13. A dog weighs 27 lb. A football player weighs 9 times as much as the dog. About how many pounds does the football player weigh?

14. Nyesha has 872 stamps in her stamp collection. Her mother has 8 times as many stamps. About how many stamps does Nyesha's mother have?

_____

_____

Test Prep

15. Alma traveled 324 mi to visit her grandmother. Kevin traveled 5 times as far to see his uncle. About how many miles did Kevin travel?

A. 150 mi   **B.** 1,500 mi   **C.** 6,000 mi   **D.** 15,000 mi

16. **Writing in Math** Lana found the exact answer to 6×623. Her exact answer was less than her estimate of 3,600. Is Lana's exact answer correct? Explain.

_____

_____

_____

_____

Mental Math

Use mental math to find each product.

1. $50 \times 3 =$ _____

2. $8 \times 82 =$ _____

3. $61 \times 5 =$ _____

4. $7 \times 29 =$ _____

5. $33 \times 4 =$ _____

6. $27 \times 9 =$ _____

7. $43 \times 7 =$ _____

8. $6 \times 68 =$ _____

9. $8 \times 92 =$ _____

10. $69 \times 3 =$ _____

11. $2 \times 34 =$ _____

12. $71 \times 8 =$ _____

13. Suppose an office building is 4 times as tall as a tree that measures 52 ft. How tall is the office building? _____

14. Suppose a baseball stadium is 6 times as wide as an equipment trailer that measures 73 feet. How wide is the baseball stadium? _____

15. **Algebra** In $n \times p = 185$, n is a two-digit number and p is a one-digit number. What numbers do n and p represent?

_____

Test Prep

16. Which of the following has a greater product than 29×8?

A. 34×5 **B.** 27×9 **C.** 38×4 **D.** 25×9

17. **Writing in Math** Explain how you would find the product of 3×75 by using the break apart method.

_____

_____

_____

Name_____

Using Arrays to Multiply

Use the array to find the partial products and the product.
Complete the calculation.

1.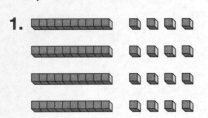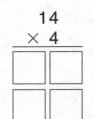

$$\begin{array}{r} 14 \\ \times\ 4 \end{array}$$

2.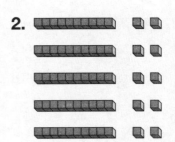

$$\begin{array}{r} 12 \\ \times\ 5 \end{array}$$

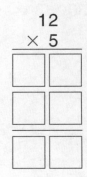

3.
$$\begin{array}{r} 17 \\ \times\ 4 \end{array}$$
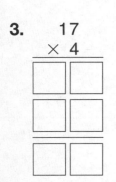

4.
$$\begin{array}{r} 25 \\ \times\ 3 \end{array}$$
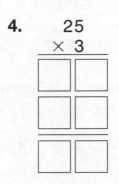

5.
$$\begin{array}{r} 21 \\ \times\ 4 \end{array}$$
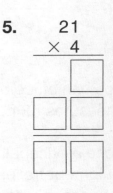

6. $4 \times 17 =$ _____

7. $5 \times 24 =$ _____

8. $3 \times 18 =$ _____

9. $5 \times 29 =$ _____

10. $23 \times 3 =$ _____

11. $21 \times 6 =$ _____

12. Clyde planted 4 rows of tomato seeds. Each row has
12 seeds. How many tomato seeds did Clyde plant? _____

Test Prep

13. Find 7×22.

    A. 54   **B.** 144   **C.** 152   **D.** 154

14. Writing in Math Write a description of an array of stickers
using the product of 3×15.

_____

_____

_____

Name_____

Multiplying Two-Digit and One-Digit Numbers

Find each product. Decide if your answer is reasonable.

1.   1 9
       $\times$ 4
    _____
     7 ☐

2.   2 3
       $\times$ 7
    _____
     ☐ 6 ☐

3.   5 1
       $\times$ 6
    _____
     ☐ 0 ☐

4.   39
      $\times$ 7

5.   48
      $\times$ 5

6.   53
      $\times$ 7

7.   29
      $\times$ 8

8. $42 \times 6 =$ _____

9. $89 \times 8 =$ _____

10. $77 \times 9 =$ _____

11. $94 \times 4 =$ _____

12. Number Sense Penny says that $4 \times 65 = 260$. Estimate to check Penny's answer. Is she right? Explain.

_____

_____

13. A large dump truck uses about 18 gal of fuel in 1 hr of work. How many gallons of fuel are needed if the truck works for 5 hours?   _____

Test Prep

14. Which of the following is a reasonable estimate for 6×82?

A. 48   **B.** 480   **C.** 540   **D.** 550

15. Writing in Math Tyrone has 6 times as many marbles as his sister Pam. Pam has 34 marbles. Louis has 202 marbles. Who has more marbles, Tyrone or Louis? Explain how you found your answer.

_____

_____

Multiplying Three-Digit and One-Digit Numbers

Find each product. Estimate for reasonableness.

1. $\begin{array}{r} 352 \\ \times\ \ \ 3 \\ \hline \end{array}$

2. $\begin{array}{r} 385 \\ \times\ \ \ 4 \\ \hline \end{array}$

3. $\begin{array}{r} 482 \\ \times\ \ \ 8 \\ \hline \end{array}$

4. $\begin{array}{r} 632 \\ \times\ \ \ 5 \\ \hline \end{array}$

5. $\begin{array}{r} 219 \\ \times\ \ \ 6 \\ \hline \end{array}$

6. $\begin{array}{r} 768 \\ \times\ \ \ 7 \\ \hline \end{array}$

7. $\begin{array}{r} 521 \\ \times\ \ \ 4 \\ \hline \end{array}$

8. $\begin{array}{r} 848 \\ \times\ \ \ 9 \\ \hline \end{array}$

9. $7 \times 211 =$ _____

10. $6 \times 517 =$ _____

If the baseball players in the table score the same number of runs each season, how many runs will

Runs Scored in 2001

Player	Runs Scored
A	128
B	113
C	142

11. Player A score in 5 seasons?

_____

12. Player C score in 8 seasons?

_____

Test Prep

13. How many bottles of water would Tim sell if he sold 212 bottles each week for 4 weeks?

    A. 800   **B.** 840   **C.** 848   **D.** 884

14. **Writing in Math** If you know that $8 \times 300 = 2,400$, how can you find 8×320? Explain.

    _____

    _____

    _____

PROBLEM-SOLVING STRATEGY

Try, Check, and Revise

Use the first try to help you make a second try. Finish solving
the problem.

1. Anton put 35 marbles equally into 5 jars. Each jar
   holds either 5 large marbles or 7 small marbles.
   What size of marbles did Anton put into the jars?

```
  5 jars
x 5 large marbles
  ──
  25

That's not enough.
```

_____

_____

_____

Try, check, and revise to solve each problem. Write the answer
in a complete sentence.

2. Lenore earned $6 per hour and Dora earned $8 per hour.
   Lenore and Dora worked the same number of hours.
   Lenore earned $54. How much did Dora earn?

_____

3. Thomas read 3 of the books.
   He read a total of 272 pages.
   Which of the books did he read?

Book	Pages
Dark Mysteries	87
History of France	146
Superhero Stories	72
Artists to Know	113

_____

_____

_____

4. Heather read 2 of the books. She also read a music book
   with 211 pages. She read a total of 429 pages. Which of
   the books did she read?

_____

_____

Choose a Computation Method

Find each product. Tell what computation method you used.

1.   4,701
   ×   6

   _____

2.   8,644
   ×   5

   _____

3.   4,698
   ×   8

   _____

4.   9,204
   ×   3

   _____

5.   5,920
   ×   4

   _____

6.   6,114
   ×   7

   _____

7.   7,100
   ×   4

   _____

8.   4,923
   ×   9

   _____

9. Mervin's Market sells about 1,250 lb of apples in 1 year. How many pounds of apples will Mervin's Market sell in 4 years?

_____

10. The airline flies 8,112 mi in 1 day. How many miles does the airline fly in 6 days?   _____

Test Prep

11. A theme park has 6 parking lots. If each of the parking lots holds 1,100 cars, how many total cars can park?

   A. 6,000 cars   **B.** 6,100 cars   **C.** 6,500 cars   **D.** 6,600 cars

12. **Writing in Math** Which method would you use to find 4,202 × 8? Explain.

_____

_____

_____

Multiplying Money

Find each product.

1. $2.48
  $\times$ 8

2. $3.82
  $\times$ 5

3. $45.86
  $\times$ 6

4. $22.72
  $\times$ 7

5. 4 × $8.23 = _____

6. 7 × $31.14 = _____

7. 9 × $25.88 = _____

8. $43.86 × 6 = _____

Find each cost.

9. 5 boxes of modeling clay

_____

10. 6 boxes of colored pencils

_____

Arts-N-Crafts	
Item	**Price per Box**
Beads $3.29	
Modeling clay $4.32	
Origami paper $7.91	
Colored pencils $2.05	

11. 4 boxes of beads

_____

12. 7 boxes of origami paper

_____

Test Prep

13. Nemo wants to buy calendars for his family. Each calendar costs $5.62. How much money do 5 calendars cost?

A. $25.10   **B.** $28.00   **C.** $28.10   **D.** $30.10

14. Writing in Math At a local restaurant, a turkey sandwich costs $6.50. An apple juice costs $1.25. Would $15.00 be enough to buy 2 sandwiches and 2 juices? Explain.

_____

_____

_____

Multiplying Three Factors

1. $2 \times 4 \times 9$ **2.** $9 \times 8 \times 3$ **3.** $4 \times 4 \times 10$

_____   _____   _____

4. $6 \times 50 \times 2$ **5.** $8 \times 60 \times 5$ **6.** $20 \times 7 \times 3$

_____   _____   _____

7. $2 \times 600 \times 5$ **8.** $80 \times 6 \times 2$ **9.** $4 \times 70 \times 4$

_____   _____   _____

10. Show three ways to find $40 \times 2 \times 5$.

_____

_____

_____

11. How many building blocks did Travis use to build his city?

_____

_____

Travis' Building Blocks
1 toy city = 4 buildings
1 building = 4 sides
1 side   = 20 blocks

Test Prep

12. How many apples would you have altogether if you have 5 apples in each of 3 bowls on each of 4 tables?

A. 60 apples   **B.** 72 apples   **C.** 81 apples   **D.** 100 apples

13. **Writing in Math** What is the cost of a truckload of sand if there are 25 bags per truckload, 10 lb of sand per bag, and each pound of sand costs $2? Show two different ways to solve the problem.

_____

_____

PROBLEM-SOLVING SKILL

Choose an Operation

Draw a picture to show the main idea. Then choose an operation and solve the problem.

1. A sack of potatoes weighs 20 lb and holds 200 potatoes. A sack of apples weighs 20 lb and holds 325 apples. How many more apples are there in a 20 lb sack?

_____

2. Shawna has 35 football cards and 5 times as many baseball cards in her sports-card collection. How many baseball cards does she have?

_____

3. A pound of peaches costs $1.29. How much does 4 lb of peaches cost?

_____

4. The first modern electronic computer, called ENIAC, was introduced in 1946. Personal home computers were not available until 28 years later. In what year were personal home computers introduced?

_____

Name_____

Paper Problems

The business section of Caitlin's newspaper lists the
performances of many stocks. There are 14 stocks listed
in every 1 in. of the stock report.

1. How many stocks are listed in 6 in. of the stock report?

   _____

   _____

2. In 1 ft of the stock report, there are 168 stocks listed. How
   many stocks are listed in 5 ft of stock reports?

   _____

   _____

The lifestyle section of Caitlin's newspaper
has a daily crossword puzzle. The puzzle
has 8 rows and 8 columns.

3. How many total spaces are in
   the crossword puzzle?

   _____

   _____

4. There are 13 blocked (or black) spaces where you cannot
   write a letter. In how many spaces can you write a letter?

   _____

   _____

5. Suppose in 1 day you bought 3 copies of the newspaper for
   $0.50 each. How much would it cost to do this for 6 days?

   _____

Name_____

Multiplying Multiples of Ten

Multiply. Use mental math.

1. $4 \times 30 =$ _____   **2.** $5 \times 90 =$ _____

3. $9 \times 200 =$ _____   **4.** $6 \times 500 =$ _____

5. $3 \times 600 =$ _____   **6.** $8 \times 6{,}000 =$ _____

7. $90 \times 70 =$ _____   **8.** $70 \times 400 =$ _____

9. $60 \times 8{,}000 =$ _____   **10.** $30 \times 800 =$ _____

11. $90 \times 5{,}000 =$ _____   **12.** $30 \times 4{,}000 =$ _____

13. Number Sense How many zeros are in the product of $60 \times 9{,}000$? Explain how you know.

_____

_____

Truck A can haul 4,000 lb in one trip. Truck B can haul 3,000 lb in one trip.

14. How many pounds can Truck A haul in 9 trips?   _____

15. How many pounds can Truck B haul in 50 trips?   _____

Test Prep

16. How many pounds can Truck A haul in 70 trips?

   A. 280   **B.** 2,800   **C.** 28,000   **D.** 280,000

17. Writing in Math There are 9 players on each basketball team in a league. Explain how you can find the total number of players in the league if there are 30 teams.

_____

_____

_____

Estimating Products

Estimate each product.

1. 38 × 29 _____   **2.** 71 × 47 _____

3. 54 × 76 _____   **4.** 121 × 62 _____

5. 548 × 28 _____   **6.** 823 × 83 _____

7. 67 × 289 _____   **8.** 183 × 34 _____

Estimate each product by finding a range.

9. 28 × 87   **10.** 673 × 85

_____   _____

The distance between San Francisco, California, and
Salt Lake City, Utah, is 752 miles.

11. Find a range for the number of   **12.** About how many miles would
miles a car would drive if it made   a car drive if it made 42 trips?
15 trips.

_____   _____

Test Prep

13. Vera has 8 boxes of paper clips. Each box has 275 paper
clips. About how many paper clips does Vera have?

A. 240   **B.** 1,600   **C.** 2,400   **D.** 24,000

14. Writing in Math A wind farm generates 330 kilowatts of
electricity each day. About how many kilowatts does the
wind farm produce in a week? Explain.

_____

_____

_____

Using Arrays to Multiply

Use the grid to draw a rectangle. Then complete the calculation.

1.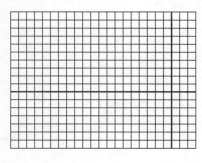

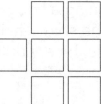

2.
$$\begin{array}{r} 3\ 1 \\ \times\ \ 1\ 9 \\ \hline \end{array}$$

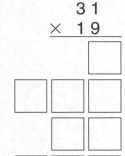

3.
$$\begin{array}{r} 2\ 6 \\ \times\ \ 2\ 2 \\ \hline \end{array}$$

4.
$$\begin{array}{r} 3\ 3 \\ \times\ \ 1\ 4 \\ \hline \end{array}$$

5. $24 \times 57 =$ _____

6. $44 \times 48 =$ _____

7. A red kangaroo can cover 40 ft in 1 jump. How many feet can the red kangaroo cover in 12 jumps? _____

Test Prep

8. Barb exercises for 14 hr in 1 week. How many hours does she exercise in 32 weeks?

A. 496 hr   **B.** 448 hr   **C.** 420 hr   **D.** 324 hr

9. Writing in Math Explain how the product of 16×34 is like the product of 6×34 plus 10×34.

Name_____

Make an Organized List

Make an organized list to solve each problem. Write each answer in a complete sentence.

1. Tonya and Lauren are designing a soccer uniform. They want to use two colors on the shirt. Their choices are green, orange, yellow, purple, blue, and silver. How many ways can they choose two colors?

_____

_____

2. Yancey collects plastic banks. He has three different banks: a pig, a cow, and a horse. How many ways can Yancey arrange his banks on a shelf?

_____

_____

3. Kevin has a rabbit, a ferret, a gerbil, and a turtle. He feeds them in a different order each day. In how many different orders can Kevin feed his pets?

_____

_____

_____

_____

Multiplying Two-Digit Numbers

1. 54
  × 17

2. 36
  × 20

3. 53
  × 12

4. 48
  × 46

5. 37
  × 83

6. 62
  × 17

7. 91
  × 49

8. 28
  × 56

9. 70
  × 39

10. 58
  × 90

11. 97
  × 42

12. 64
  × 88

13. A carton holds 24 bottles of juice. How many juice bottles are in 15 cartons?

_____

14. How much do 21 bushels of sweet corn weigh?

_____

15. How much do 18 bushels of asparagus weigh?

_____

Vegetable	Weight of 1 Bushel
Asparagus	24 lb
Beets	52 lb
Carrots	50 lb
Sweet corn	35 lb

16. How much more do 13 bushels of beets weigh than 13 bushels of carrots?

_____

Test Prep

17. Which of the following is a reasonable answer for 92 × 98?

   A. 1,800   **B.** 9,000   **C.** 10,000   **D.** 90,000

18. **Writing in Math** Garth is multiplying 29 × 16. He has 174 after multiplying the ones and 290 after multiplying the tens. Explain how Garth can find the final product.

_____

Multiplying Greater Numbers

1. 242
× 30

2. 194
× 19

3. 306
× 22

4. 420
× 82

5. 324
× 38

6. 832
× 69

7. 493
× 75

8. 968
× 27

9. 828
× 34

10. 335
× 45

11. 616
× 37

12. 494
× 65

13. **Number Sense** Is 44,722 a reasonable answer for
59 × 758? Explain.

_____

_____

14. How many pencils are in 27 boxes?

_____

Supplies	Per Box
Pencils	144
Pens	115

15. How many pens are in 42 boxes?

_____

Test Prep

16. Hailey sold 122 bottles of water in 1 week. About how
many bottles could she sell in 19 weeks?

   A. 1,000   **B.** 1,800   **C.** 2,400   **D.** 3,000

17. **Writing in Math** How could you use the product
10 × 414 = 4,140 to find the product of 12 × 414?

_____

Name_____

Choose a Computation Method

Multiply. Tell what method you used.

1.   50
        ×90   _____

        _____

2.   324
        × 42   _____

        _____

3.   84
        ×39   _____

        _____

4.   600
        × 40   _____

        _____

5.   537
        × 88   _____

        _____

6.   224
        × 21   _____

        _____

How many books would you expect

7. Store B to sell in 10 weeks?

_____

8. Store A to sell in 20 weeks?

_____

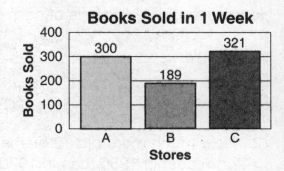

Books Sold in 1 Week

9. How many more books would you
expect to be sold in 6 weeks in
Store C than in Store A?

_____

Test Prep

10. Nathan has 20 friends coming to his party. If each friend
brings 20 snacks, how many snacks are there?

A. 400   **B.** 800   **C.** 1,000   **D.** 2,000

11. Writing in Math Explain when you would choose a calculator to multiply.

_____

_____

Multiplying Money

1. $1.26
    × 40

2. $2.30
    × 14

3. $3.96
    × 18

4. $4.21
    × 33

5. $5.54
    × 26

6. $2.28
    × 67

7. $3.37
    × 34

8. $4.82
    × 42

9. **Number Sense** Margo bought 36 shirts that cost $6.86 each. Which of the following is most likely to be the product, $24.69, $246.96, or $2,469.60? Explain.

_____

_____

How much did 42 bushels of corn cost in

10. 1970? _____

11. 2000? _____

12. How much more did 19 bushels of corn cost in 1980 than in 1990?

_____

Price of Corn

Year	Per Bushel
1970	$1.33
1980	$3.11
1990	$2.28
2000	$1.85

Test Prep

13. The fourth-grade class rented 24 pairs of skates at the ice rink. Each pair cost $2.45. How much did it cost to rent the skates?

    A. $5.88   **B.** $49.00   **C.** $58.80   **D.** $62.48

14. **Writing in Math** Craig multiplied 43 × $5.46 and got an answer of $234.78. Do you agree? Explain.

_____

_____

Name _____

Writing to Explain

Write to explain.

1. Bonnie completed a tennis tournament. She received 5 points for each set she won. Complete the table and use the pattern to find the number of points she earned on the 4th and 5th days. Explain how the number of points earned increases as the number of sets won increases.

Day	1	2	3	4	5
Sets Won	2	3	4	5	6
Points	10	15	20		

_____

_____

2. Use the pictograph to find the difference between the number of Jazz and Country CDs sold in January. Show your computation neatly. Explain how you found your answer.

January CD Sales

Jazz	○○○○○○
Classical	○○○○
Country	○○○

Each ○ = 50 CDs.

_____

_____

_____

3. Copy the table and use the pattern to complete it. Explain how the number of students changes as the number of classrooms changes.

Classrooms	2	4	6	8	10
Students	48	96	144		

_____

_____

_____

The Magazine

A magazine has 11 editors who supervise the writing of different parts of the magazine. Each managing editor has 28 workers.

1. Estimate how many total workers there are. Explain your estimate.

   _____

   _____

2. Find the number of workers there are
   for the 11 editors.   _____

The magazine company publishes 56 issues each year.
How many issues will the company publish in

3. 8 years? _____

4. 15 years? _____

5. 27 years? _____

Each magazine costs $4.59 per issue. How much would it cost for

6. 6 issues? _____

7. 11 issues? _____

8. 23 issues? _____

A subscriber receives the magazine each week at home in the mail. Subscribers pay $2.04 per issue. How much does the magazine cost for subscribers to get

9. 24 issues? _____

10. 52 issues? _____

11. A newsstand sells 716 issues of the magazine
    per week. How many issues does the
    newsstand sell in 1 year?   _____

Using Patterns to Divide Mentally

Divide. Use mental math.

1. $250 \div 5 =$ _____

2. $1,400 \div 2 =$ _____

3. $300 \div 5 =$ _____

4. $1,600 \div 4 =$ _____

5. $240 \div 8 =$ _____

6. $36,000 \div 4 =$ _____

7. $16,000 \div 2 =$ _____

8. $270 \div 3 =$ _____

9. $4,200 \div 7 =$ _____

10. $640 \div 8 =$ _____

11. $2,000 \div 5 =$ _____

12. $320 \div 8 =$ _____

13. $12,000 \div 2 =$ _____

14. $1,600 \div 8 =$ _____

The fourth grade performed a play based on the story of Cinderella. There was one chair for each person present.

15. On Friday, 140 people came to the play. The chairs in the auditorium were arranged in 7 equal rows. How many chairs were in each row? _____

16. There were 8 equal rows set up for Saturday's performance. There were 240 people at the play on Saturday. How many chairs were in each row? _____

Test Prep

17. Which is the quotient of $56,000 \div 8$?

    A. 400   **B.** 4,000   **C.** 700   **D.** 7,000

18. **Writing in Math** Explain why the following answer is not correct: $1,000 \div 5 = \underline{2,000}$.

    _____

    _____

    _____

Estimating Quotients

Estimate each quotient. Tell whether you found
an overestimate or an underestimate.

1. $82 \div 4$ _____

2. $580 \div 3$ _____

3. $96 \div 5$ _____

4. $811 \div 2$ _____

5. $194 \div 6$ _____

6. $207 \div 7$ _____

7. $282 \div 4$ _____

8. $479 \div 8$ _____

9. Jacqui is writing a book. If she needs to
write 87 pages in 9 days, about how
many pages will she write each day? _____

10. Wade wants to give 412 of his marbles to
10 of his friends. If he gives each friend
the same number of marbles, about
how many will each friend receive? _____

Test Prep

11. Which is the best estimate for $502 \div 6$?

A. 60   **B.** 70   **C.** 80   **D.** 90

12. Writing in Math You are using division to determine how
much whole wheat flour to use in a bread recipe. Is an
estimated answer good enough?

_____

_____

Name_____

Dividing with Remainders

Divide. You may use counters or pictures to help.

1. $4\overline{)27}$ **2.** $6\overline{)32}$ **3.** $7\overline{)17}$ **4.** $9\overline{)29}$

5. $8\overline{)27}$ **6.** $3\overline{)27}$ **7.** $5\overline{)28}$ **8.** $4\overline{)35}$

9. $2\overline{)19}$ **10.** $7\overline{)30}$ **11.** $3\overline{)17}$ **12.** $9\overline{)16}$

If you arrange these items into equal rows, tell how many will be in each row and how many will be left over.

13. 26 shells into 3 rows   _____

14. 19 pennies into 5 rows   _____

15. 17 balloons into 7 rows   _____

16. **Number Sense** Ms. Nikkel wants to divide her class of 23 students into 4 equal teams. Is this reasonable? Why or why not?

_____

_____

Test Prep

17. Which is the remainder for the quotient of $79 \div 8$?

    A. 7   **B.** 6   **C.** 5   **D.** 4

18. **Writing in Math** Pencils are sold in packages of 5. Explain why you need 6 packages in order to have enough for 27 students.

_____

_____

Name_____

Two-Digit Quotients

Use place-value blocks or draw pictures. Tell how many CDs are in each case and how many are left over.

1. 60 CDs
   5 cases _____

2. 72 CDs
   4 cases _____

3. 93 CDs
   8 cases _____

Divide. You may use place-value blocks or pictures to help.

4. $9\overline{)97}$ **5.** $3\overline{)67}$ **6.** $6\overline{)80}$ **7.** $5\overline{)97}$

8. $2\overline{)54}$ **9.** $7\overline{)54}$ **10.** $8\overline{)92}$ **11.** $2\overline{)53}$

12. Number Sense Mr. Brooks brought a box of 66 acorns to class. Can he give 3 acorns to each of the 23 students in his class? Why or why not?

_____

_____

_____

Test Prep

13. Which is the quotient of 45 ÷ 4?

   A. 10 R5   **B.** 11 R1   **C.** 11 R4   **D.** 12 R2

14. Writing in Math Explain how you can find the quotient of 84 ÷ 4.

_____

_____

_____

Dividing Two-Digit Numbers

1.

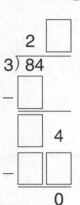

2.

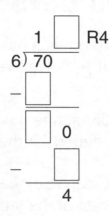

3.

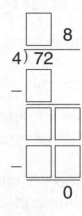

4. 2)72   **5.** 5)86   **6.** 7)94   **7.** 3)39

8. 8)99   **9.** 5)87   **10.** 2)96   **11.** 3)43

Mrs. Thomas is planning to provide snacks for 96 fourth graders when they go on a field trip to the aquarium. Each student will receive 1 of each snack. How many packages of each snack does Mrs. Thomas need?

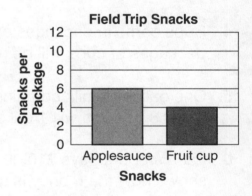

12. fruit cups   _____

13. applesauce   _____

Test Prep

14. Which is the remainder of 124 ÷ 18?

   A. 12   **B.** 16   **C.** 18   **D.** 20

15. Writing in Math Explain how to find the number of leftover pencils if Wendy wants to share 37 pencils with 9 people.

_____

_____

_____

Name_____

Interpreting Remainders

The fourth-grade class is going camping as a nature field trip. There are 85 students going on the trip. Solve the following questions with this information.

1. There are 47 girls in the group. If each tent holds 3 people, how many tents are needed for the girls? _____

2. The group will take 4 buses that can each carry 20 children and their gear. The rest of the students will ride in the school van. How many students will ride in the van? _____

3. The teachers and parents will make 4 large pots of soup for dinner. About how many servings will each pot need to contain to feed all the students, 4 teachers, and 6 parents? _____

4. Cups come in packages of 20. How many packages of cups will be needed for this meal? _____

5. One gallon of milk contains 128 fluid oz. How many 8 oz cups will 1 gal contain? _____

6. Each student pays $10.00 for the field trip. The chart shows how the money is used. If the leftover money is used for maintaining the camping equipment, how much does each student contribute for equipment?

   Costs per Student

Camping fee	$2.00
Bus service	$3.50
Food	$3.75

   _____

Name_____

Dividing Three-Digit Numbers

1.

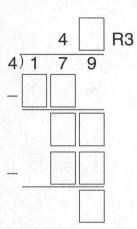

```
    4 □ R3
4)1 7 9
- □□
  □□
- □□
   □
```

2.

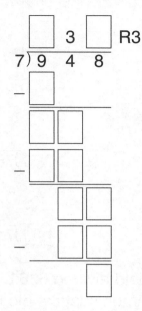

```
  □ 3 □ R3
7)9 4 8
- □
  □□
- □□
  □□
  □□
- □□
   □
```

3.

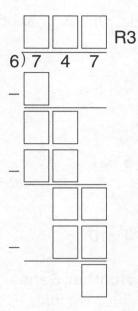

```
  □□□ R3
6)7 4 7
- □
  □□
- □□
  □□
- □□
   □
```

4. 7)698   **5.** 8)747   **6.** 2)329   **7.** 9)411

8. 3)198   **9.** 2)587   **10.** 5)975   **11.** 6)573

12. Algebra When 475 is divided by *n*, the quotient
is 25. Solve for *n*.

_____

13. Algebra When 289 is divided by *x*, the quotient
is 96 R1. Solve for *x*.

_____

Test Prep

14. Yvonne needs to distribute 345 stickers to 8 classrooms.
How many stickers will each classroom get?

A. 53   **B.** 44   **C.** 43   **D.** 38

15. Writing in Math Write and solve a word problem for $245 \div 7$.

_____

_____

_____

Zeros in the Quotient

Divide. Check your answer.

1. 3)921 **2.** 4)834 **3.** 5)549 **4.** 2)611

5. 6)627 **6.** 8)824 **7.** 7)762 **8.** 5)535

9. 4)810 **10.** 6)121 **11.** 7)712 **12.** 9)936

13. Number Sense When Donald divided 636 by 6, his quotient was 16. What common mistake did he make?

_____

The fourth graders in Clifton's classroom used computer games to practice their math skills. Each student's score was the same in each round.

14. Clifton scored 918 points in 9 rounds of math facts. How many points did he score in each round? _____

15. Brionne scored 654 points in 6 rounds. How many points did she score in each round? _____

Test Prep

16. Which is the quotient of 617 ÷ 3?

A. 203 R2   **B.** 205   **C.** 205 R1   **D.** 205 R2

17. Writing in Math In Patricia's class, 7 students need to share 714 building blocks to make a building model. Each student needs an equal number of blocks. Patricia thinks each student should have 100 blocks. Is this the best plan? Explain.

_____

Dividing Money Amounts

Divide. Check your answer.

1. 4)$8.12

2. 3)$1.20

3. 5)$6.55

4. 2)$9.68

5. 7)$7.21

6. 9)$8.19

7. 6)$4.74

8. 8)$9.52

Use the table at the right for Exercises 9 and 10. Find the cost of one of each type of tropical fish.

9. Neon barb

_____

10. Guppy

_____

Pete's Pets

Fish	Price
Guppies	6 for $1.44
Neon barbs	3 for $3.99
Tetras	3 for $4.98
Zebra danio	3 for $2.19
Black snail	$0.99 each

11. Marcus bought 6 cans of fish food for $7.74. How much did he spend per can?   _____

Test Prep

12. If James bought 5 trading cards for $5.25, how much did each card cost?

A. $0.88   **B.** $0.99   **C.** $1.00   **D.** $1.05

13. **Writing in Math** Explain how you can use the fact $620 \div 4 = 155$ to find the cost of each bottle of water, if the price is $6.20 for 4 bottles.

_____

_____

_____

_____

Name_____

Write a Number Sentence

Using a Number Sentence to Solve Problems Solve the
number sentence. Write the answer in a complete sentence.

1. McKinley Elementary School is holding its
   annual science fair. There are 140 projects to
   be displayed. There is room for 5 projects on
   each table. How many tables are needed to
   display all the projects?

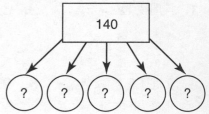

_____

_____

Writing a Number Sentence to Solve Problems Draw a picture
to show the main idea for each problem. Then write a number
sentence. Solve. Write the answer in a complete sentence.

2. Stanley's science fair project is on recycling.
   As part of the project, he and his friends
   collected 45 lb of aluminum cans and
   redeemed them at the recycling center. They
   received $0.31 per pound. How much did
   they receive for all their cans?

_____

_____

3. Brittany's project showed the size of the
   planet Jupiter as compared to Earth. She
   found that the diameter of Jupiter was
   about 11 times greater than the diameter
   of Earth. If her model of Earth has a
   diameter of 2 in., how large should the
   diameter of her model of Jupiter be?

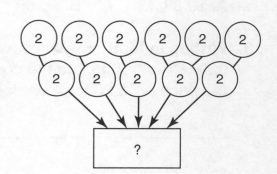

_____

_____

Divisibility Rules

Test each number to see if it is divisible by 2, 3, 5, 9, and 10.

1. 15 _____

2. 45 _____

3. 48 _____

4. 60 _____

5. 198 _____

6. 375 _____

7. 720 _____

8. 682 _____

9. Name four ways Mr. Yancey can divide his class of 20 into equal groups.

_____

_____

10. Derrick has a collection of 85 baseball cards that he wants to put into a binder. He wants to put them on pages that hold 9 cards each. Will each of the pages be filled? How do you know?

_____

_____

Test Prep

11. Which of the following numbers is divisible by 2, 3, 5, 9, and 10?

A. 255   **B.** 309   **C.** 450   **D.** 535

12. **Writing in Math** A school bus can hold a maximum of 66 students. How do you know you can equally put 3 students in each seat?

_____

_____

Finding Averages

Find the average, or mean, of each set of data.

1. 6, 9, 4, 5 _____

2. 4, 8, 2, 7, 4 _____

3. 17, 25, 15 _____

4. 47, 36, 44, 29 _____

5. 9, 6, 7, 4, 3, 7 _____

6. 124, 233, 156 _____

7. 25, 16, 12, 42, 20 _____

8. 425, 125, 542 _____

9. **Number Sense** Could the average of three numbers be one of those three numbers? Give an example.

_____

_____

Use the table at the right for 10–14.

Find the average score for each bowler.

10. Ali _____

11. Brenda _____

12. Caitlin _____

13. Joseph _____

Bowling Scores

Bowler	Game		
	1	2	3
Ali	107	67	114
Brenda	112	115	124
Caitlin	98	125	137
Joseph	94	87	122

Test Prep

14. Which is the average of the following test scores: 98, 96, 100, 93, 83?

    A. 90   **B.** 94   **C.** 96   **D.** 470

15. **Writing in Math** In the set 42, 43, 51, 52, and 44, explain why the average will be in the 40s.

_____

_____

Dividing by Multiples of 10

Divide. Use mental math.

1. $360 \div 40 =$ _____ 2. $450 \div 90 =$ _____ 3. $270 \div 30 =$ _____

4. $630 \div 70 =$ _____ 5. $1,600 \div 40 =$ _____ 6. $1,000 \div 20 =$ _____

7. $250 \div 50 =$ _____ 8. $490 \div 70 =$ _____ 9. $1,200 \div 60 =$ _____

10. $400 \div 80 =$ _____ 11. $2,100 \div 70 =$ _____ 12. $1,800 \div 30 =$ _____

13. **Number Sense** If $270 \div 90 = 3$ and $2,700 \div 90 = 30$, what is $270,000 \div 90$? _____

The whooping crane is being reintroduced to the midwestern United States. The birds fly from Wisconsin to Florida in the fall.

14. Suppose a group of cranes covered the 1,200 mi trip south in about 20 flying days. How far did they fly per day? _____

15. In the spring, the birds flew the return trip back north in only 10 days. How many times as fast did the birds fly on their return trip? _____

16. Suppose that one day the flock covered 80 mi in 2 hr. How many miles per hour were the birds flying?

_____

Test Prep

17. Which is the quotient of $5,400 \div 60$?

    A. 50   **B.** 60   **C.** 90   **D.** 900

18. **Writing in Math** Would it be quicker to use a calculator or to use mental math to answer Exercise 17? Why?

_____

_____

_____

Dividing with Two-Digit Divisors

Estimate each quotient. Then divide.

1. 84 ÷ 22 _____

2. 271 ÷ 53 _____

3. 379 ÷ 42 _____

4. 294 ÷ 61 _____

5. 29)‾1‾6‾7‾

6. 34)‾2‾9‾6‾

7. 57)‾3‾7‾9‾

8. 76)‾2‾4‾7‾

9. 55)‾1‾7‾9‾

10. 82)‾3‾9‾6‾

11. Ms. Nicholas brought 189 blue beads and 189 white beads so that her class could make bracelets. It takes 42 beads to make a bracelet. How many bracelets could they make? _____

12. Mr. Barkley is helping students make candles using wax and empty milk cartons. Mr. Barkley carefully melted 160 oz of wax. If each of the 26 students makes a candle, about how many ounces will each candle weigh? _____

Test Prep

13. Trisha scored 568 points in 71 basketball games. How many points did she score per game?

A. 9 points **B.** 8 R41 points **C.** 8 R22 points **D.** 8 points

14. Writing in Math Explain why the remainder of any division problem must be smaller than the divisor.

_____

_____

_____

_____

Name_____

The Divisions of Space

Solve. Write your answer in a complete sentence.

1. Astronauts eat 3 meals per day. An astronaut may require about 2,400 calories each day. If an astronaut eats the same amount of calories each meal, how many calories does the astronaut consume at each meal?

_____

_____

2. Astronauts use a space suit so they can space walk outside of a shuttle or station. A space suit's oxygen and power need to be recharged in the space shuttle after 8 hr of space walking. How many times does the space suit need to be recharged if used for 192 hr?

_____

_____

3. An astronaut is scheduled to sleep for 480 min each day. If an astronaut is sleeping in a space shuttle that is orbiting Earth, he could see the sun rise every 45 min. How many times could an astronaut see the sun rise during his scheduled sleep time?

_____

_____

4. What was the average distance from Earth for the space shuttle *Atlantis* from Wednesday until Saturday?

_____

_____

Distance from Earth for *Atlantis*

Day	Distance
Wednesday	278 mi
Thursday	323 mi
Friday	350 mi
Saturday	253 mi

Name_____

Relating Solids and Plane Figures

Complete the table.

Solid Figure	Number of Faces	Number of Edges	Number of Vertices
1. Square Pyramid			
2. Cube			
3. Triangular Prism			

Identify the solid that best describes each object.

4.

_____

5.

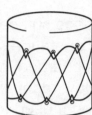

_____

6.

_____

7. How many total faces does a rectangular prism have?

_____

Test Prep

8. Which solid does the figure represent?

A. Rectangular pyramid   **C.** Rectangular prism

B. Cylinder   **D.** Square pyramid

9. Writing in Math Explain the difference between a plane figure and a solid figure.

_____

_____

_____

Polygons

Draw an example of each polygon. How many sides and
vertices does each one have?

1. Square   **2.** Octagon   **3.** Hexagon

_____   _____   _____

The map shows the shapes
of buildings in Polygon Park.
Identify the polygons that
are lettered.

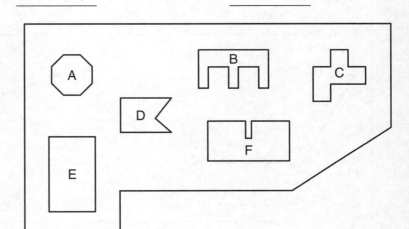

4. A

_____

5. D

_____

6. C   **7.** B

_____   _____

8. E   **9.** F

_____   _____

Test Prep

10. Which is the point where sides meet in a polygon?

A. Edge   **B.** Endpoint   **C.** Side   **D.** Vertex

11. Writing in Math Describe two polygons by the number of
vertices and sides each has.

_____

Lines, Line Segments, Rays, and Angles

Use geometric terms to describe what is shown. Be as specific as possible.

1.

_____

2.

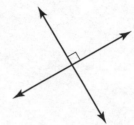

_____

3.

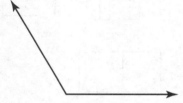

_____

4.

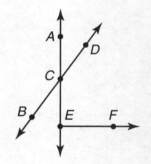

_____

5. Name two lines.

_____

6. Name two obtuse angles.

_____

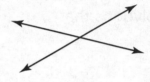

Test Prep

7. Which is the geometric term for ∠HJK?

  A. Acute angle   **C.** Right angle

  B. Obtuse angle   **D.** Straight angle

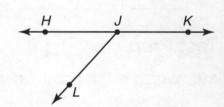

8. **Writing in Math** Describe an acute angle.

_____

_____

Name_____

Triangles and Quadrilaterals

P 8-4

Classify each triangle by its sides and then by its angles.

1.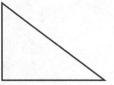

_____

2.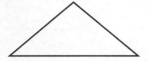

_____

3.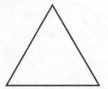

_____

Write the name of each quadrilateral.

4.

_____

5.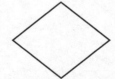

_____

Test Prep

6. Which is a triangle with one right angle?

A. Scalene triangle   **C.** Right triangle

B. Obtuse triangle   **D.** Acute triangle

7. Writing in Math Explain why a square can never be a trapezoid.

_____

_____

_____

Circles

Use geometric terms to describe what is shown on each circle.

1.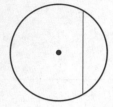

_____

2.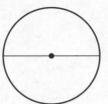

_____

3.

_____

Find the length of the diameter of each circular object.

4.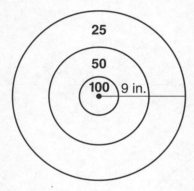

_____

5.

_____

Test Prep

6. A CD has a radius of 6 cm. Which is its diameter?

A. 3 cm   **B.** 12 cm   **C.** 18 cm   **D.** 12 in.

7. Writing in Math What is the relationship between the diameter and the radius of a circle?

_____

_____

_____

_____

Congruent Figures and Motions

Do the figures in each pair appear to be congruent? If so,
tell if they are related by a flip, slide, or turn.

1.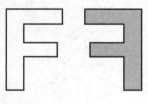

_____

2.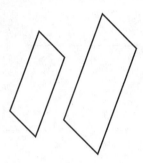

_____

3.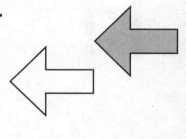

_____

4.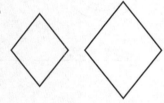

_____

5.

_____

6.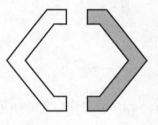

_____

Test Prep

7. Which figure described could be
congruent to this rectangle?

A. A quadrilateral with equal sides   **C.** A quadrilateral with equal angles

B. A rectangle with equal sides   **D.** A triangle with equal sides

8. Writing in Math Describe how four turns can put a figure
in its original position.

_____

_____

_____

Name _____

Symmetry

How many lines of symmetry does each figure have?

1.

_____

2.

_____

3.

_____

4.

_____

5.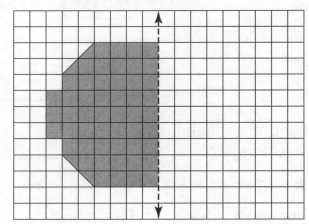

_____

6.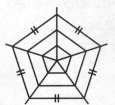

_____

7. Finish the drawing to make it symmetric.

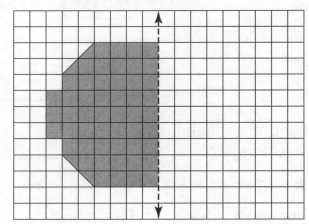

Test Prep

8. How many lines of symmetry does a rhombus that is not a square have?

A. 0   **B.** 1   **C.** 2   **D.** 3

9. **Writing in Math** Explain why a square is always symmetric.

_____

_____

_____

Similar Figures

Do the figures in each pair appear to be similar? If so, are they also congruent?

1.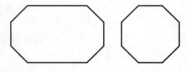

2.

3.

_____

4.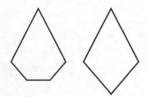

5.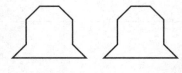

6.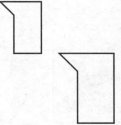

_____

Test Prep

7. Which pair of figures is similar and congruent?

A.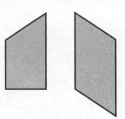

C.

B.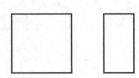

D.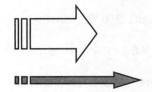

8. Writing in Math Explain why similar figures are not always congruent.

_____

_____

_____

Name_____

Writing to Describe

Write two statements to describe how each pair of figures
are alike or different. Use geometric terms.

1.

_____

_____

_____

2.

_____

_____

_____

Test Prep

3. Which statement does NOT correctly
   describe the figures?

    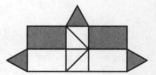

   A. The figures are similar.

   B. Both figures have five sections.

   C. One figure has 3 triangles and the other has 7 triangles.

   D. The shading of the figures is different.

4. **Writing in Math** Describe how a baseball and a basketball are alike.

_____

_____

104 Use with Lesson 8-9.

Name_____

Perimeter

Find the perimeter of each figure.

1.
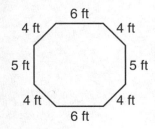
6 ft
4 ft 4 ft
5 ft 5 ft
4 ft 4 ft
6 ft

_____

2.
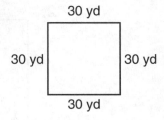
30 yd
30 yd 30 yd
30 yd

_____

3.
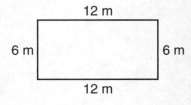
12 m
6 m 6 m
12 m

_____

4.
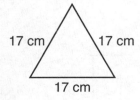
17 cm 17 cm
17 cm

_____

5.
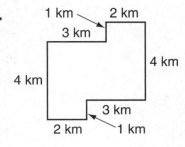
1 km 2 km
3 km
4 km
4 km
3 km
2 km 1 km

_____

6.
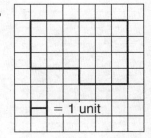
= 1 unit

_____

7. What is the perimeter around the bases?

_____

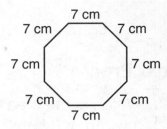
90 ft 90 ft
90 ft 90 ft

Test Prep

8. Which is the perimeter of this figure?

A. 77 cm   **B.** 63 cm

C. 56 cm   **D.** 28 cm

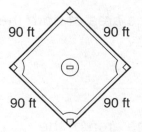
7 cm
7 cm 7 cm
7 cm 7 cm
7 cm 7 cm
7 cm

9. Writing in Math Explain how you can use
multiplication to find the perimeter of a square.

_____

_____

_____

Name_____

Area

Find the area of each figure.

1.
5 in.

5 in.

_____

2.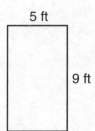
5 ft

9 ft

_____

3.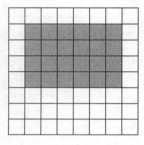

_____

4.
2 cm

2 cm

4 cm

6 cm

2 cm

4 cm

2 cm

_____

5. What is the area of both the bedrooms?

_____

6. What is the area of the whole house?

_____

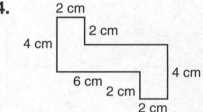

32 ft

20 ft

20 ft

30 ft

20 ft | Bedroom

Living space

28 ft

20 ft | Bedroom

Garage | 30 ft

Test Prep

7. Which is the area of a rectangle with a length of 26 cm and a width of 34 cm?

A. 992 cm   **B.** 884 cm   **C.** 720 cm   **D.** 324 cm

8. **Writing in Math** Explain how you would find the length of one side of a square if the area is 16 square units.

_____

Name_____

Act It Out

Solve each problem. Write the answer in a complete sentence.

1. The Wilsons have 12 yd of fence for their garden. What are the length and width of the garden if it has the greatest possible area?

_____

2.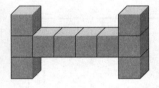

   The town of Mount Harris needs to build another bridge over Franklin Creek. If the second bridge is exactly the same as the first bridge, how many cube units are needed to build the second bridge?

_____

3. Joshua wants to build a fort in his backyard. He has 10 pieces of wood that are each 6 ft long. If Joshua arranges the wood into a rectangle to make the greatest area, what is the area of the fort?

_____

4. The Community Center wants to separate the basement of their activity hall into two rooms. One room will be used for storage and the other will have space for table tennis. The entire basement is a rectangle with a length of 48 ft and a width of 12 ft. The storage room must have an area of 144 ft. What is the perimeter and area of the table tennis room?

_____

_____

Name_____

Volume

Find the volume of each figure.

1.

_____

2.
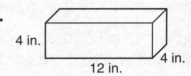
4 in. 12 in. 4 in.

_____

3.
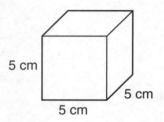
5 cm
5 cm
5 cm

_____

4.
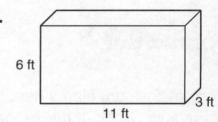
6 ft
11 ft
3 ft

_____

5. A rectangular prism has a length of
7 cm, a width of 4 cm, and a height of
3 cm. What is the volume of the prism?   _____

6. **Reasoning** The length of an edge of a
cube is 5 ft. What is the total volume of
two cubes of the same size?   _____

7. If a cube has a volume of 64 cubic units,
how long is each edge?   _____

Test Prep

8. What is the volume of a cube that has an edge of 7 yd?

   A. 343 cubic yd   **B.** 98 cubic yd   **C.** 49 cubic yd   **D.** 21 cubic yd

9. **Writing in Math** If you know that a rectangular prism has a
length of 256 m and a width of 192 m, can you find its
volume? Explain your answer.

_____

_____

PROBLEM-SOLVING APPLICATION P 8-14

Native American Math

1. Some Native American tribes used to play a game of skill in which players had to throw a lance through the center of a rolling hoop. What is the diameter of the hoop?

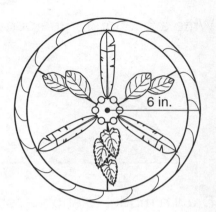

_____

2. The Plains tribe lived in tepees. What solid figure best describes a tepee?

_____

3.

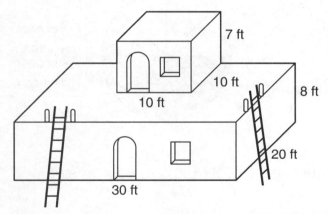

The Pueblo tribe lived in homes called pueblos. These houses were made of mud and brick and were built on top of each other like modern apartment buildings. People used ladders to get to the different levels. What is the total volume of the house and its upper room?

_____

4. To build an igloo, the Inuit of northern Canada use blocks of hard packed snow. If someone asked you to make a rectangular prism 7 blocks long, 5 blocks wide, and 4 blocks high, how many blocks would you need?

_____

Name _____

Parts of a Region

Write a fraction for the part of the region below that is shaded.

1.

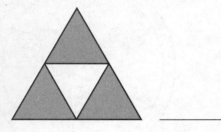

_____

2.

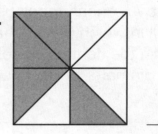

_____

Draw a model to show each fraction.

3. $\frac{2}{4}$

4. $\frac{10}{25}$

5. What fraction of the pizza is cheese?

_____

6. What fraction of the pizza is mushroom?

_____

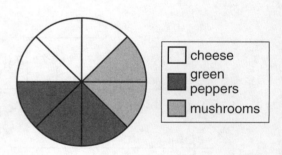

cheese
green peppers
mushrooms

7. Number Sense Is $\frac{1}{4}$ of 12 greater than $\frac{1}{4}$ of 8? Explain your answer.

_____

_____

Test Prep

8. A region has 12 equal squares. Which is the number of squares in $\frac{1}{3}$ of the region?

A. 3   **B.** 4   **C.** 6   **D.** 9

9. Writing in Math Explain why $\frac{1}{2}$ of Region A is not larger than $\frac{1}{2}$ of Region B.

_____

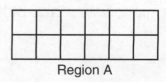

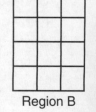

Region A   Region B

Name_____

Parts of a Set

What fraction of each set is shaded?

1.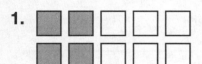

2.

3.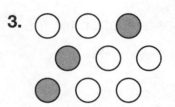

_____   _____   _____

4. 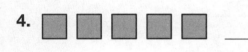 _____

5.

_____

Draw a picture to show each fraction as part of a set.

6. $\frac{3}{6}$ 7. $\frac{2}{5}$

8. **Number Sense** $\frac{5}{5}$ of the models that Brian has are airplanes. How many are cars?

_____

Test Prep

9. What fraction of the half-circles is shaded?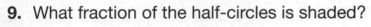

   A. $\frac{1}{8}$ **B.** $\frac{1}{2}$ **C.** $\frac{3}{4}$ **D.** $\frac{2}{8}$

10. **Writing in Math** Frank said that $\frac{1}{2}$ of the squares to the right are shaded. Is he correct? Explain.

_____

_____

Name _____

Fractions, Length, and the Number Line

Write a fraction for the part of each length that is shaded.

1. |▬▬|—|—|—|

_____

2. |▬▬▬▬|—|—|—|—|—|—|—|—|

_____

3. |▬▬▬▬▬▬▬▬|

_____

4. |▬▬▬|—|—|

_____

5. |▬▬▬|—|—|—|

_____

6. |▬▬▬▬▬▬|—|

_____

Which fraction should be written at each point?

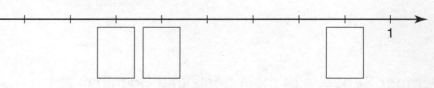

7. A _____

8. B _____

9. C _____

Reasoning Write the missing fractions.

10.

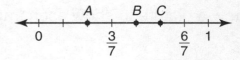

Test Prep

11. Which fraction could go on a number line instead of 1?

    A. $\frac{0}{7}$ **B.** $\frac{5}{7}$ **C.** $\frac{7}{7}$ **D.** $\frac{1}{2}$

12. **Writing in Math** Explain why point A could be written as either $\frac{1}{2}$ or $\frac{4}{8}$.

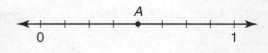

_____

_____

_____

  Use with Lesson 9-3.

Estimating Fractional Parts

Estimate the fractional part of each that is shaded.

1.

2.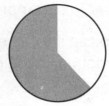

3.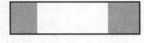

_____   _____   _____

4. **Number Sense** Is $\frac{1}{6}$ a reasonable estimate for the shaded part in the region to the right? Explain.

_____

_____

Estimate the fraction that should be written at each point.

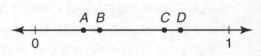

5. *A* _____   6. *B* _____   7. *C* _____   8. *D* _____

Test Prep

9. Part of the region to the right is shaded. Which is the best estimate?

   A. $\frac{3}{3}$ **B.** $\frac{2}{3}$ **C.** $\frac{1}{3}$ **D.** $\frac{0}{3}$

10. **Writing in Math** Explain how you estimated the shaded region in Exercise 9.

_____

_____

_____

_____

Name_____

Draw a Picture

Solve each problem. Write the answer in a complete sentence.

1. Three friends divided a veggie pizza into 12 slices. If they
   divide the pizza equally, what fraction of the pizza would
   each friend get?

   _____

2. Mark is making a quilt with his grandmother. Each row
   of the quilt has 6 squares. There are 8 rows. $\frac{1}{2}$ of the
   squares are blue. How many blue squares are in the quilt?

   _____

3. Jane pulled weeds in the garden 7 times. She was paid $5
   each time she pulled weeds for less than 1 hr and $6 each
   time she pulled weeds for more than 1 hr. If Jane received
   $39, how many times did she pull weeds for more than 1 hr?

   _____

   _____

4. Neil needs to cut 3 long boards into 9 smaller
   boards. The first is 10 ft, the second is 16 ft, and
   the third is 18 ft. The table lists the smaller
   boards Neil needs. Use a drawing to show how
   he can divide the 3 boards so there is no waste.

Length of Board	Number Needed
4 ft	3
5 ft	4
6 ft	2

10 ft

16 ft

18 ft

Name_____

Equivalent Fractions

Multiply or divide to find equivalent fractions.

1.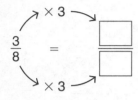

2.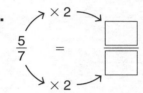

3.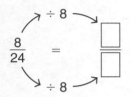

4.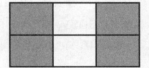

5. $\frac{11}{22}$ _____

6. $\frac{1}{5}$ _____

7. $\frac{5}{8}$ _____

8. $\frac{12}{30}$ _____

9. Number Sense Write two fractions that name the shaded part in the figure to the right. Explain how your fractions are equivalent.

_____

_____

Test Prep

10. Which is NOT an equivalent fraction to $\frac{2}{3}$?

A. $\frac{4}{6}$ **B.** $\frac{6}{9}$ **C.** $\frac{9}{12}$ **D.** $\frac{10}{15}$

11. Writing in Math 12 counters are arranged in 4 dishes as shown. How could you rearrange the shaded or white counters to clearly show two equivalent fractions? What are the fractions?

    1   2   3   4

_____

_____

_____

Fractions in Simplest Form

Write each fraction in simplest form. If it is in simplest form, write *simplest form*.

1. $\frac{7}{8}$ _____

2. $\frac{2}{14}$ _____

3. $\frac{3}{9}$ _____

4. $\frac{7}{7}$ _____

5. $\frac{5}{30}$ _____

6. $\frac{20}{36}$ _____

7. $\frac{7}{15}$ _____

8. $\frac{16}{22}$ _____

9. $\frac{8}{12}$ _____

10. $\frac{27}{36}$ _____

11. **Number Sense** What fraction of the region to the right is shaded? Write your answer in simplest form. Explain how you know.

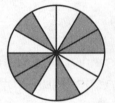

_____

_____

Give each fraction in simplest form. What fraction of the farm to the right is

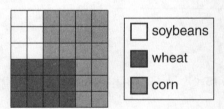

soybeans
wheat
corn

12. soybeans? _____

13. wheat? _____

14. corn? _____

Test Prep

15. Which fraction is in simplest form?

   A. $\frac{6}{24}$ B. $\frac{7}{24}$ C. $\frac{8}{24}$ D. $\frac{9}{24}$

16. **Writing in Math** Is $\frac{11}{33}$ written in simplest form? How do you know?

_____

_____

Using Number Sense to Compare Fractions

Write > or < for each $\bigcirc$. You may use fraction strips to help.

1. $\frac{1}{2} \bigcirc \frac{3}{13}$　　　　2. $\frac{8}{9} \bigcirc \frac{5}{9}$　　　　3. $\frac{3}{8} \bigcirc \frac{11}{22}$

4. $\frac{3}{3} \bigcirc \frac{7}{8}$　　　　5. $\frac{3}{5} \bigcirc \frac{1}{3}$　　　　6. $\frac{1}{4} \bigcirc \frac{2}{4}$

7. $\frac{5}{6} \bigcirc \frac{5}{8}$　　　　8. $\frac{7}{12} \bigcirc \frac{4}{5}$　　　　9. $\frac{3}{7} \bigcirc \frac{6}{7}$

10. **Number Sense** Explain how you know that $\frac{21}{30}$ is greater than $\frac{2}{3}$.

_____

_____

_____

11. Tina completed $\frac{2}{3}$ of her homework before dinner.
George completed $\frac{4}{7}$ of his homework before dinner.
Who completed a greater fraction of homework?　_____

12. Jackson played a video game for $\frac{1}{6}$ hr. Hailey played
a video game for $\frac{1}{3}$ hr. Who played the video game
for a greater amount of time?　_____

Test Prep

13. Which fraction is greater than $\frac{3}{4}$?

A. $\frac{5}{9}$　　　　B. $\frac{17}{24}$　　　　C. $\frac{15}{20}$　　　　D. $\frac{7}{9}$

14. **Writing in Math** James says that $\frac{5}{5}$ is greater than $\frac{99}{100}$.
Is he correct? Explain.

_____

_____

_____

Name _____

Comparing and Ordering Fractions

Compare. Write >, <, or = for each ◯.

1. $\frac{2}{5}$ ◯ $\frac{5}{10}$ 2. $\frac{11}{16}$ ◯ $\frac{5}{8}$ 3. $\frac{4}{5}$ ◯ $\frac{8}{9}$

4. $\frac{3}{6}$ ◯ $\frac{6}{12}$ 5. $\frac{2}{7}$ ◯ $\frac{3}{10}$ 6. $\frac{1}{4}$ ◯ $\frac{2}{11}$

7. **Number Sense** Without multiplying, Emily knew that $\frac{4}{9}$ was greater than $\frac{4}{10}$. Explain how she knew.

_____

_____

_____

Order the numbers from least to greatest.

8. $\frac{4}{15}, \frac{2}{5}, \frac{1}{3}$ _____   9. $\frac{4}{10}, \frac{2}{8}, \frac{1}{5}$ _____

10. $\frac{1}{9}, \frac{7}{8}, \frac{5}{6}$ _____   11. $\frac{3}{9}, \frac{1}{4}, \frac{5}{12}$ _____

12. $\frac{13}{16}, \frac{5}{8}, \frac{2}{8}$ _____   13. $\frac{1}{2}, \frac{7}{12}, \frac{4}{10}$ _____

Test Prep

14. Which fraction is greater than $\frac{1}{3}$?

   A. $\frac{3}{6}$ B. $\frac{11}{36}$ C. $\frac{1}{4}$ D. $\frac{1}{12}$

15. **Writing in Math** Explain how you know that $\frac{31}{40}$ is greater than $\frac{3}{4}$, but less than $\frac{4}{5}$.

_____

_____

_____

_____

118 Use with Lesson 9-9.

Mixed Numbers and Improper Fractions

Write each mixed number as an improper fraction.

1. $3\frac{2}{5}$ _____

2. $6\frac{1}{4}$ _____

3. $2\frac{1}{12}$ _____

4. $2\frac{7}{9}$ _____

Write each improper fraction as a mixed number or whole number.

5. $\frac{12}{5}$ _____

6. $\frac{27}{9}$ _____

7. $\frac{32}{3}$ _____

8. $\frac{20}{12}$ _____

9. Number Sense Matt had to write $3\frac{8}{24}$ as an improper fraction. Write how you would tell Matt the easiest way to do so.

_____

_____

_____

10. Jill has 4 granola bars. Each bar weighs $\frac{2}{3}$ oz. Write the weight of Jill's granola bars as an improper fraction and as a mixed number. _____

11. Nick had $1\frac{3}{4}$ gal of milk. How many pints of milk does Nick have? (Hint: There are 8 pt in 1 gal.) _____

Test Prep

12. Which is NOT an improper fraction equal to 8?

A. $\frac{24}{3}$ **B.** $\frac{49}{7}$ **C.** $\frac{56}{7}$ **D.** $\frac{64}{8}$

13. Writing in Math Write three different improper fractions that equal $4\frac{2}{3}$.

_____

Name_____

Comparing Mixed Numbers

Compare. Write >, <, or = for each $\bigcirc$.

1. $3\frac{1}{4}$ $\bigcirc$ $2\frac{7}{8}$ 2. $2\frac{9}{16}$ $\bigcirc$ $3\frac{1}{5}$ 3. $1\frac{7}{8}$ $\bigcirc$ $1\frac{3}{4}$ 4. $5\frac{3}{8}$ $\bigcirc$ $5\frac{1}{2}$

5. $3\frac{15}{16}$ $\bigcirc$ $4\frac{1}{9}$ 6. $3\frac{2}{3}$ $\bigcirc$ $3\frac{2}{14}$ 7. $5\frac{2}{3}$ $\bigcirc$ $5\frac{3}{5}$ 8. $1\frac{9}{10}$ $\bigcirc$ $1\frac{8}{9}$

Reasoning Write the missing numbers as mixed numbers.
Write the fractional part in simplest form.

9.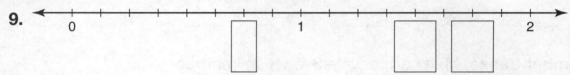

10.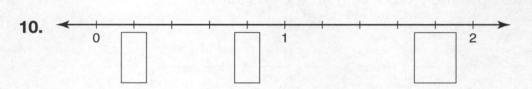

11. Jack and Callie are helping Mr. Harris by washing
chalkboards at school. Before they take a lunch break,
Jack has washed $3\frac{1}{3}$ chalkboards and Callie has washed
$3\frac{5}{6}$ chalkboards. Who has washed more chalkboards?   _____

Test Prep

12. Which is greater than $4\frac{2}{3}$?

   A. $4\frac{5}{8}$ **B.** $4\frac{3}{4}$ **C.** $4\frac{2}{5}$ **D.** $4\frac{1}{3}$

13. **Writing in Math** Explain how to find whether or not $2\frac{1}{3}$ is
greater than $\frac{9}{4}$.

_____

_____

_____

_____

_____

Name_____

Circle Graphs

Julie counted the 24 trees on her block. She wrote the data in a table and then made this circle graph.

Trees on Block

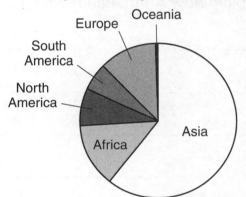

What fraction of the trees are

1. oaks? ———

2. elms or maples? ———

3. marked as "other"? ———

4. The table shows the type of table that Julie made to make her circle graph. Because you know that there are 12 oak trees on Julie's block, you can complete the entire table.

Tree	Number
Oaks	
Elms	
Maples	
Other	

5. About what fraction of the world's population lives in Asia?

_____

Population by Continent-2001

6. Name 2 continents that have about $\frac{1}{4}$ of the world's population.

_____

Test Prep

7. Two parts of a circle graph are each $\frac{1}{3}$ of the circle. The other two parts are equal in size. What fraction of the graph is each of the smaller parts?

   A. $\frac{1}{6}$ **B.** $\frac{1}{4}$ **C.** $\frac{1}{3}$ **D.** $\frac{1}{2}$

8. **Writing in Math** John counted what people were drinking as he walked to school. He saw 3 people drinking coffee, 3 drinking juice, and 2 drinking water. John wants to put the data in a circle graph. How many equal parts should he divide his circle into? Explain your answer.

_____

_____

PROBLEM-SOLVING SKILL
Writing to Explain

1. Mary has 23 marbles. $\frac{7}{23}$ of the marbles are yellow and $\frac{13}{23}$ of the marbles are blue. The rest of the marbles are green. How many marbles are green? Explain how you know.

_____

_____

_____

_____

2. Adam wants to compare the fractions $\frac{2}{5}$, $\frac{1}{6}$, and $\frac{1}{3}$. He wants to order them from least to greatest and rewrite them so they all have the same denominator. Explain how Adam can rewrite the fractions.

_____

_____

_____

_____

3. Adam used the three fractions to make a circle graph and colored each a different color. What fraction of the graph is not colored? Explain your answer.

_____

_____

_____

_____

Name_____

Fractional Orchards

Trees in an Orchard

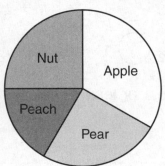

Tree	Acres
Apple	8
Pear	6
Peach	4
Nut	6

The circle graph and table show the acres for each tree grown in an orchard.

What fractional part of the orchard is

1. apple trees? _____

2. pear and peach trees combined? _____

3. nut trees? _____

4. NOT peach trees? _____

5. Explain how you knew what each fractional part was.

_____

_____

_____

_____

6. The part of the orchard for nut trees is divided into 3 equal parts for 3 different types of nut trees. What fractional part of the whole orchard is each nut tree? Explain.

_____

_____

_____

_____

Name_____

Estimating Fraction Sums

Write > or < for each ◯.

1. $\frac{2}{6} + \frac{1}{3}$ ◯ 1 2. $\frac{2}{3} + \frac{4}{5}$ ◯ 1 3. $\frac{3}{4} + \frac{7}{10}$ ◯ 1 4. $\frac{2}{7} + \frac{1}{6}$ ◯ 1

5. $\frac{4}{10} + \frac{3}{8}$ ◯ 1 6. $\frac{8}{10} + \frac{5}{6}$ ◯ 1 7. $\frac{1}{4} + \frac{3}{12}$ ◯ 1 8. $\frac{3}{7} + \frac{1}{16}$ ◯ 1

Estimate to decide whether each sum is greater than 1 or less than 1. If you cannot tell, explain why.

9. $\frac{2}{3} + \frac{5}{6}$ _____

_____

10. $\frac{1}{16} + \frac{8}{20}$ _____

_____

11. $\frac{8}{9} + \frac{1}{7}$ _____

_____

12. Three quarters are worth $\frac{3}{4}$ of a dollar and 4 dimes are worth $\frac{4}{10}$ of a dollar. Are 3 quarters and 4 dimes worth more than or less than a dollar?

13. A half dollar is worth $\frac{1}{2}$ of a dollar and 5 nickels are worth $\frac{5}{20}$ of a dollar. Are 1 half dollar and 5 nickels worth more than or less than a dollar?

Test Prep

14. Which of the following is greater than 1?

A. $\frac{1}{2} + \frac{1}{3}$ B. $\frac{7}{8} + \frac{6}{10}$ C. $\frac{2}{5} + \frac{5}{12}$ D. $\frac{6}{18} + \frac{3}{7}$

15. **Writing in Math** Explain how to estimate if $\frac{3}{5} + \frac{5}{8}$ is greater than or less than 1.

_____

_____

Adding Fractions with Like Denominators

Find each sum.

1. $\frac{7}{10} + \frac{2}{10} =$ _____

2. $\frac{4}{5} + \frac{4}{5} =$ _____

3. $\frac{1}{6} + \frac{2}{6} =$ _____

4. $\frac{3}{8} + \frac{2}{8} =$ _____

5. $\frac{2}{5} + \frac{2}{5} =$ _____

6. $\frac{3}{6} + \frac{1}{6} =$ _____

7. $\frac{4}{6} + \frac{4}{6} =$ _____

8. $\frac{2}{3} + \frac{2}{3} =$ _____

9. $\frac{1}{8} + \frac{1}{8} =$ _____

10. $\frac{4}{12} + \frac{6}{12} =$ _____

11. **Number Sense** Cindy says that when two numerators add up to the same number as the two like denominators, the answer will always be 1. Is she correct? Explain.

_____

_____

_____

There are 8 pencils in a box: 2 are red, 2 are blue, 3 are yellow, and 1 is brown. What fraction of the pencils are

12. red?   13. yellow?   14. red and blue combined?

_____   _____   _____

Test Prep

15. Which is the sum of $\frac{8}{12} + \frac{1}{12}$?

    A. $\frac{9}{24}$ **B.** $\frac{5}{12}$ **C.** $\frac{7}{12}$ **D.** $\frac{9}{12}$

16. **Writing in Math** Explain how you know your answer to Exercise 10 is reasonable.

_____

_____

Name_____

Adding Fractions with Unlike Denominators

Find each sum.

1. $\frac{1}{3} + \frac{1}{4} =$ _____

2. $\frac{1}{5} + \frac{1}{3} =$ _____

3. $\frac{5}{8} + \frac{1}{4} =$ _____

4. $\frac{3}{10} + \frac{5}{6} =$ _____

5. $\begin{array}{r} \frac{3}{4} \\ + \frac{4}{5} \\ \hline \end{array}$

6. $\begin{array}{r} \frac{1}{12} \\ + \frac{3}{4} \\ \hline \end{array}$

7. $\begin{array}{r} \frac{1}{8} \\ + \frac{1}{4} \\ \hline \end{array}$

8. $\begin{array}{r} \frac{2}{3} \\ + \frac{2}{9} \\ \hline \end{array}$

9. $\begin{array}{r} \frac{1}{7} \\ + \frac{2}{5} \\ \hline \end{array}$

10. $\begin{array}{r} \frac{5}{6} \\ + \frac{1}{3} \\ \hline \end{array}$

11. $\begin{array}{r} \frac{1}{14} \\ + \frac{2}{7} \\ \hline \end{array}$

12. $\begin{array}{r} \frac{1}{3} \\ + \frac{4}{15} \\ \hline \end{array}$

A class was asked how many siblings each student had. The results are listed in the table.

Number of Siblings

0	1	2	3 or more
$\frac{11}{30}$	$\frac{1}{3}$	$\frac{1}{5}$	$\frac{1}{10}$

13. What fraction of the class has fewer than 2 siblings?

_____

14. What fraction of the class has more than 1 sibling? _____

Test Prep

15. Which is the sum of $\frac{5}{7} + \frac{1}{2}$?

A. $\frac{3}{7}$ B. $\frac{6}{7}$ C. $1\frac{1}{7}$ D. $1\frac{3}{14}$

16. **Writing in Math** Is Amanda's work correct? Explain why or why not.

_____

_____

_____

$$\begin{array}{r} \frac{3}{4} = \frac{3}{12} \\ + \frac{1}{3} = \frac{4}{12} \\ \hline \frac{7}{12} \end{array}$$

Subtracting Fractions with Like Denominators

Find each difference.

1. $\frac{5}{6} - \frac{4}{6} =$ _____

2. $\frac{4}{6} - \frac{1}{6} =$ _____

3. $\frac{4}{5} - \frac{2}{5} =$ _____

4. $\frac{7}{8} - \frac{2}{8} =$ _____

5. $\frac{3}{4} - \frac{2}{4} =$ _____

6. $\frac{4}{5} - \frac{1}{5} =$ _____

7. $\frac{7}{9} - \frac{1}{9} =$ _____

8. $\frac{9}{12} - \frac{7}{12} =$ _____

9. $\begin{array}{r} \frac{5}{6} \\ - \frac{1}{6} \\ \hline \end{array}$

10. $\begin{array}{r} \frac{7}{8} \\ - \frac{3}{8} \\ \hline \end{array}$

11. $\begin{array}{r} \frac{2}{5} \\ - \frac{1}{5} \\ \hline \end{array}$

12. $\begin{array}{r} \frac{9}{15} \\ - \frac{4}{15} \\ \hline \end{array}$

13. Mr. Brown had $\frac{4}{5}$ tbsp of salt. He used $\frac{1}{5}$ tbsp of salt in a recipe. How much is left? _____

14. In Mrs. DeLong's class, $\frac{5}{9}$ of her class are boys and $\frac{4}{9}$ of her class are girls. What is the difference between the fraction of boys and the fraction of girls? _____

15. **Estimation** Is $\frac{11}{12} - \frac{7}{12}$ more than or less than $\frac{1}{2}$? Explain.

_____

Test Prep

16. Which is the difference of $\frac{7}{15} - \frac{3}{15}$?

   A. $\frac{4}{30}$ **B.** $\frac{4}{15}$ **C.** $\frac{1}{2}$ **D.** 4

17. **Writing in Math** Frank says that $\frac{6}{12} - \frac{1}{12}$ is less than $\frac{1}{2}$. Is he correct? Explain your answer.

_____

Name_____

Subtracting Fractions with Unlike Denominators

Find each difference. Simplify if necessary.

1. $\frac{5}{6} - \frac{1}{3} =$ _____

2. $\frac{4}{5} - \frac{2}{3} =$ _____

3. $\frac{7}{8} - \frac{1}{2} =$ _____

4. $\frac{11}{12} - \frac{3}{4} =$ _____

5. $\frac{7}{12} - \frac{1}{3} =$ _____

6. $\frac{1}{2} - \frac{2}{7} =$ _____

7. $\frac{2}{3} - \frac{1}{4} =$ _____

8. $\frac{5}{8} - \frac{1}{3} =$ _____

9. $\quad \frac{7}{10}$
$-\ \frac{2}{5}$
_____

10. $\quad \frac{9}{10}$
$-\ \frac{1}{2}$
_____

11. $\quad \frac{5}{9}$
$-\ \frac{2}{5}$
_____

12. $\quad \frac{7}{12}$
$-\ \frac{1}{10}$
_____

The background of the flag of Chile is $\frac{1}{6}$ blue, $\frac{1}{3}$ white, and $\frac{1}{2}$ red.

13. How much more of the flag is red than blue?

_____

White
Blue
Red

14. How much more of the flag is white than blue?

_____

15. What fraction of the flag is blue and
white combined?

_____

Test Prep

16. Which is the difference of $\frac{1}{2} - \frac{1}{16}$?

A. $\frac{1}{16}$

B. $\frac{1}{8}$

C. $\frac{3}{8}$

D. $\frac{7}{16}$

17. Writing in Math Explain how you know that $\frac{7}{8} - \frac{1}{4}$ will be more than $\frac{1}{2}$.

_____

_____

Name_____

Use Logical Reasoning

Solve each problem. Write the answer in a complete sentence.

1. Jennifer and her four friends, Anna, Debra, Mary, and Sue, were born in different months of the same year. The girls were born in January, March, April, September, and December. None of the girls were born in a month that begins with the same letter as their first name. Sue is the youngest, and Debra is the oldest. Jennifer was born in September. In what month was Mary born?

_____

2. What figure comes next?

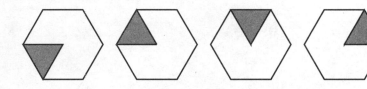

3. John, Ben, and Thomas each brought a different kind of sandwich for lunch. The boys had bologna, ham, and turkey sandwiches. John does not like ham, and Thomas brings bologna every day. What kind of sandwich did each boy bring for lunch?

_____

_____

_____

_____

4. Randall has a meeting this afternoon. He knows it is on the half hour, but he cannot remember which half hour. The meeting is after 1 P.M. and before 6 P.M. The sum of the digits in the time is 7. What time is Randall's meeting?

_____

Name_____

Length and Customary Units

Estimate first. Then, measure each length to the nearest inch.

1. ├──────────────────────────┤   _____

2. ├───────────┤   _____

Choose the most appropriate unit to measure the length of each. Write in., ft, yd, or mi.

3. boat _____   4. wallet _____

5. soccer field _____   6. finger bandage _____

7. computer cable _____   8. train route _____

9. nose _____   10. sea _____

11. Use a ruler to find the perimeter of the triangle.

_____

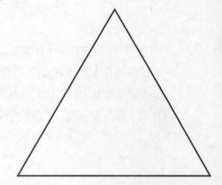

12. Eileen needs 9 ft of fabric to make a skirt. How many yards of fabric does she need?

_____

Test Prep

13. Which unit would be most appropriate for measuring the length of a barn?

   A. Inches   **B.** Pounds   **C.** Yards   **D.** Miles

14. **Writing in Math** Explain how you would decide which unit is best for measuring your math book.

_____

_____

Name_____

Fractions of an Inch

Measure each to the nearest $\frac{1}{2}$ inch, $\frac{1}{4}$ inch, and $\frac{1}{8}$ inch.

1.  _____, _____, _____

2.  _____, _____, _____

3.  _____, _____, _____

4. Draw a line segment that is $4\frac{5}{8}$ in. long to the nearest $\frac{1}{8}$ inch and $4\frac{3}{4}$ in. to the nearest $\frac{1}{4}$ inch.

What is the combined diameter of

5. 2 pennies to the nearest $\frac{1}{4}$ inch?

_____

6. 1 nickel and 1 dime to the nearest $\frac{1}{8}$ inch?

_____

Diameter of Coin to Nearest $\frac{1}{8}$ in.	
Penny	$\frac{3}{4}$ in.
Nickel	$\frac{7}{8}$ in.
Dime	$\frac{3}{4}$ in.
Quarter	1 in.

Test Prep

7. Find the length to the nearest $\frac{1}{4}$ in.

├────────────┤

   A. 1 in.   **B.** $1\frac{1}{4}$ in.   **C.** $1\frac{1}{2}$ in.   **D.** 2 in.

8. **Writing in Math** Use the information in the table above. Which coin would be useful to measure an object to the nearest inch? Explain.

_____

_____

_____

Capacity and Customary Units

Choose the most appropriate unit or units to measure the capacity of each. Write tsp, tbsp, fl oz, c, pt, qt, or gal.

1. teacup _____

2. juice box _____

3. motor oil _____

4. pepper in a recipe _____

5. carton of creamer _____

6. lake _____

7. **Number Sense** Would a teaspoon be a good way to measure the capacity of a milk carton? Explain.

_____

_____

8. A refreshment jug for the baseball team holds 20 gal of water. To make an energy drink, 1 c of mix is used for every 2 gal of water. How many cups of the mix are needed to fill the jug with energy drink? _____

Test Prep

9. Which unit has the greatest capacity?

    A. Tablespoon   **B.** Quart

    C. Pint   **D.** Teaspoon

10. **Writing in Math** Cassidy says that capacity is the same as the amount. Do you agree? Explain why or why not.

_____

_____

_____

_____

Weight and Customary Units

Choose the most appropriate unit to measure the weight of each. Write oz, lb, or T.

1. truck _____
2. can of vegetables _____

3. person _____
4. desk _____

5. trailer full of bricks _____
6. cup of flour _____

7. box of paper _____
8. CD _____

9. **Reasoning** Would a scale that is used to weigh food be the best tool to weigh concrete blocks? Explain why or why not.

_____

_____

_____

10. Jen wants to weigh her cat. Should she weigh the cat with ounces, pounds, or tons? _____

11. What unit would you use to measure the weight of your house? _____

Test Prep

12. Which animal would it be appropriate to measure in ounces?

   A. Mouse   **B.** Elephant   **C.** Horse   **D.** Cow

13. **Writing in Math** Dezi says that there are more ounces in 1 T than there are pounds. Do you agree? Explain.

_____

_____

_____

Name_____

Changing Units and Comparing Measures

Find each missing number.

1. 2 ft = _____ in.   **2.** 8 qt = _____ pt

3. 2 gal = _____ qt   **4.** 9 ft = _____ yd

5. 64 oz = _____ lb   **6.** 10,560 ft = _____ mi

7. 20 T = _____ lb   **8.** 4 lb, 6 oz = _____ oz

Compare. Write > or < for each $\bigcirc$.

9. 20 pt, 2 c $\bigcirc$ 12 qt   **10.** 10 lb $\bigcirc$ 200 oz

11. 13 ft, 6 in. $\bigcirc$ 5 yd   **12.** 100 in. $\bigcirc$ 2 yd

13. 3 gal $\bigcirc$ 10 qt   **14.** 9 oz $\bigcirc$ 9 lb

15. How many inches long is the longest car?

_____

16. How many ounces does the lightest car weigh?

Car Records

Lightest car	21 lb
Heaviest car	7,353 lb
Longest car	100 ft

_____

Test Prep

17. How many fluid ounces are in 6 c?

A. 32   **B.** 40   **C.** 48   **D.** 54

18. **Writing in Math** Explain why you cannot convert fluid ounces to pounds.

_____

_____

Exact Answer or Estimate

For 1–4, tell whether an exact answer is needed or if an estimate is enough. Then solve.

1. You have 100 lb of green beans. Each canning jar holds 14 oz of the beans. You have 100 jars. Do you have enough jars to hold all the beans?

_____

_____

Grace is making a dress to enter as a craft fair project. The pattern says that she needs 6 yd of fabric, 1 spool of thread, and 8 one-inch buttons.

2. Grace has 20 ft of fabric that she really likes. Is there enough to make the dress?

_____

_____

3. The buttons that Grace likes are $4.25 for a package of 4 buttons. The right color thread is $2.35. If Grace pays for the supplies with a $20.00 bill, how much change should she receive?

_____

_____

4. You need to add 2 gal of apple juice to a fruit punch. You only have a container that measures quarts. How many quarts should you add?

_____

_____

Name_____

Measurements Abound!

Solve each problem. Write your answer in a complete sentence.

1. Ted has 20 ft of rope and Lou has 42 ft of rope. They need to have at least 12 yd of rope between the two of them. Do they have enough? Explain your answer.

   _____

   _____

2. Arnold, Cathy, Derrick, and Eldon each have a different pet. They have a dog, a cat, a bird, and an iguana. Arnold is allergic to anything with fur. Cathy's pet can say some words, and likes to eat sunflower seeds. Derrick does not have a cat. What kind of animal is Eldon's pet?

   _____

Christie runs every morning before school. This week she ran $\frac{2}{3}$ mi each on Monday, Wednesday, and Thursday. She ran $\frac{1}{2}$ mi on Tuesday and $\frac{7}{9}$ mi on Friday.

3. How far did Christie run on Monday, Wednesday, and Thursday combined?

   _____

   _____

4. Christie wants to run at least 3 mi each week. Did she meet her goal this week? Explain how you decided.

   _____

   _____

   _____

   _____

Name_____

Decimals and Fractions

Write a fraction and a decimal for the part of each grid that is shaded.

1.

_____

2.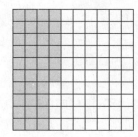

_____

Write each number as a decimal.

3. $\frac{1}{10}$ _____

4. $\frac{4}{5}$ _____

5. $3\frac{1}{2}$ _____

6. $1\frac{1}{50}$ _____

7. $\frac{11}{20}$ _____

8. $\frac{19}{100}$ _____

Write each decimal as a fraction or mixed number, in simplest form.

9. 0.77 _____

10. 0.6 _____

11. 3.75 _____

12. 2.9 _____

13. 36.36 _____

14. 6.65 _____

Kari and Timothy made origami swans and timed each other.
Kari finished her swan in 15.04 sec. Timothy finished his swan
in 17.82 sec. Write a mixed number to show how many seconds
it took each of them.

15. Kari _____

16. Timothy _____

Test Prep

17. Which fraction has the same value as 0.15?

   A. $\frac{3}{10}$ **B.** $\frac{3}{15}$ **C.** $\frac{3}{20}$ **D.** $\frac{3}{25}$

18. Writing in Math Explain how saying the decimal can help
you to write the decimal as a fraction.

_____

_____

Decimal Place Value

Write each number in standard form.

1. Two and three tenths _____

2. 200 + 8 + 0.5 + 0.06 _____

Write the word form and tell the value of the underlined digit for each number.

3. 2.1<u>9</u> _____

_____

4. 40.<u>6</u>2 _____

_____

5. Number Sense How many tenths are there in twenty hundredths? _____

To make one quarter, the cost is 4.29 cents. It costs 1.88 cents to make one dime. Write the word form for the number of cents it costs to make one of each coin.

6. quarter _____

7. dime _____

Test Prep

8. Which is 60 + 5 + 0.09 in standard form?

A. Sixty-five and nine hundredths   **B.** 65.09

C. 65.9   **D.** 659

9. Writing in Math Explain how to write eight and nineteen hundredths in standard form.

_____

_____

Name_____

Comparing and Ordering Decimals P 11-3

Compare. Write >, <, or = for each ◯.

1. 0.31 ◯ 0.41

2. 1.9 ◯ 0.95

3. 0.09 ◯ 0.1

4. 2.70 ◯ 2.7

5. 0.81 ◯ 0.79

6. 2.12 ◯ 2.21

Order the numbers from least to greatest.

7. 0.37, 0.41, 0.31

8. 1.16, 1.61, 6.11

_____

_____

9. 7.9, 7.91, 7.09, 7.19

10. 1.45, 1.76, 1.47, 1.67

_____

_____

Margaret has three cats. Sophie weighs 4.27 lb, Tigger weighs 6.25 lb, and Ghost weights 4.7 lb.

11. Which cat has the greatest weight? _____

12. Which cat weighs the least? _____

Test Prep

13. Which group of numbers is ordered from least to greatest?

  A. 0.12, 1.51, 0.65

  B. 5.71, 5.4, 0.54

  C. 0.4, 0.09, 0.41

  D. 0.05, 0.51, 1.5

14. **Writing in Math** Darrin put the numbers 7.25, 5.27, 7.52, and 5.72 in order from greatest to least. Is his work correct? Explain.
7.25, 7.52, 5.72, 5.27

_____

_____

Rounding Decimals

Round each number to the nearest whole number.

1. 15.2 _____ **2.** 0.79 _____ **3.** 1.50 _____ **4.** 6.47 _____

5. 10.23 _____ **6.** 2.75 _____ **7.** 9.32 _____ **8.** 32.58 _____

Round each number to the nearest tenth.

9. 5.62 _____ **10.** 11.47 _____

11. 0.73 _____ **12.** 1.88 _____

13. Number Sense What is the greatest decimal with hundredths that will round to 0.5 when rounded to the nearest tenth? _____

For each age group in the data file, round the part of the population to the nearest tenth.

14. under 18

_____

15. over 64

_____

U.S. Population by Age, 2000

Age Group	Part
Under 18	0.26
18 to 64	0.62
Over 64	0.12

Test Prep

16. Which number below is 8.3 when rounded to the tenths place?

A. 7.35 **B.** 8.27 **C.** 8.35 **D.** 8.39

17. Writing in Math Explain how to round 1.342 to the nearest tenth.

_____

_____

_____

_____

Estimating Decimal Sums and Differences

Estimate each sum or difference.

1. 1.45 + 0.6 _____   **2.** 8.91 + 1.16 _____   **3.** 7.09 − 5.11 _____

4. 6.59 − 3.84 _____   **5.** 8.54 + 9.01 _____   **6.** 6.11 − 0.15 _____

7.   18.05   **8.**   11.45   **9.**   8.65   **10.**   9.50
       +   0.85   −   0.9   −   5.1   +   6.8

11. Reasoning Cheryl had $86.51. She bought 6 cases of fruit drink and had $50.67 left. About how much did Cheryl pay for each case of fruit drink?

_____

12. Jean walked 19.87 mi last week, 17.15 mi the week before, and 18.92 mi this week. About how many miles has Jean walked in the 3 weeks?

_____

13. William drives 14.81 mi to work each day. Kathy drives 2.6 mi to work each day. About how much farther does William drive each day?

_____

Test Prep

14. Which is the best estimate for the sum of 22.36 + 19.6?

A. 41   **B.** 42   **C.** 43   **D.** 44

15. Writing in Math Kayla needs $15.00 to buy a CD. She has $8.18 in her wallet, $3.19 in her pocket, and $5.42 in her piggy bank. Does Kayla have enough? Explain.

_____

_____

_____

Using Grids to Add and Subtract Decimals

Add or subtract. You may use grids to help.

1. $0.12 + 0.56 =$ _____

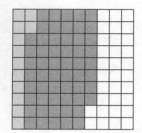

2. $0.27 - 0.09 =$ _____

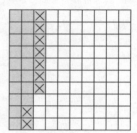

3. $0.86 + 0.54 =$ _____

4. $1.27 + 0.75 =$ _____

5. $0.93 - 0.25 =$ _____

6. $1.07 - 0.61 =$ _____

7. $1.13 - 1.02 =$ _____

8. $0.28 + 1.96 =$ _____

9. Number Sense Is the difference of $1.45 - 0.12$ less than or greater than 1? _____

10. A bottle of nail polish holds 0.8 oz. A bottle of perfume holds 0.45 oz. How many more ounces does a bottle of nail polish hold? _____

Test Prep

11. Add.
$1.18 + 1.86 =$

A. 2.04　　　　**B.** 2.94　　　　**C.** 3.04　　　　**D.** 3.14

12. Writing in Math Explain how you can use a grid to subtract $1.65 - 0.98$.

_____

_____

_____

_____

Name_____

Adding and Subtracting Decimals

1. 4.52
    + 8.61

2. 52.36
    + 9.74

3. 7.54
    − 4.64

4. 92.56
    − 13.8

5. $1.54 + 5.67 =$ _____

6. $1.56 − 0.42 =$ _____

7. $0.64 − 0.08 =$ _____

8. $92.22 + 64.53 =$ _____

9. $65.12 − 37.88 =$ _____

10. $73.12 + 77.69 =$ _____

11. $0.54 − 0.48 =$ _____

12. $0.61 + 0.88 =$ _____

13. $37.8 − 18.27 =$ _____

14. $11.94 + 7.19 =$ _____

15. There are two records for the greatest distance traveled by a model car in 24 hr. The larger scale model car traveled 305.94 mi, and the smaller scale model car traveled 213.07 mi. How many more miles did the larger car travel in 24 hr? _____

Sara and Jessica are twins. At birth, Sara weighed 5.42 lb and Jessica weighed 6.8 lb.

16. How much was their combined weight? _____

17. How much more did Jessica weigh than Sara? _____

Test Prep

18. Which is the difference of $8.97 − 7.8$?

    A. 0.17   **B.** 0.89   **C.** 1.17   **D.** 1.89

19. **Writing in Math** Heather added $9.42 + 6.3$. Is her answer correct? Explain.

    9.42
    + 6.3
    ――――
    10.05

_____

_____

_____

Name_____

Solve a Simpler Problem

Solve each problem. Write the answer in a complete sentence.

1. A grid is built using toothpicks. Each square of the grid uses one toothpick on each side. The grid formed is 12 units long and 1 unit high. How many toothpicks are needed to make the grid?

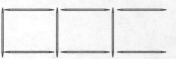

_____

2. At the end of the volleyball season, the 4 top teams hold a tournament. Each team plays each other team twice. How many games are played at the tournament altogether?

_____

3. Ben is cutting a round piece of bread dough into equal pie-shaped sections. If he keeps the circle together and makes cuts across the diameter, how many sections will he have when he has made 6 cuts?

_____

4. Doris bought 2 magazines for $1.79 each. Her dad had given her $2.50 for cleaning the car, and she already had saved $3.88. How much did Doris have left after she bought the magazines?

_____

5. Norman is folding a square piece of paper. Each fold he makes divides the folded paper in half. When he unfolds the paper, it is divided into equal sections. How many sections will there be if Norman has folded the paper 8 times?

_____

Name_____

Length and Metric Units

Estimate first. Then find each length to the nearest centimeter.

1. ├──────────────────────────┤   _____

2. ├────────┤   _____

Choose the most appropriate unit to measure each. Write mm, cm, dm, m, or km.

3. width of a house

   _____

4. distance across Lake Erie

   _____

5. width of a thumbtack

   _____

6. thickness of a phone book

   _____

Find each missing number.

7. 10 mm = _____ cm   8. 10 cm = _____ dm   9. 1 m = _____ dm

10. **Number Sense** Which would you be more
    likely to measure in centimeters, a fish tank
    or a swimming pool?   _____

11. Which is longer, a 12 cm pencil or a 1 dm pen?   _____

12. Find the area of a square with sides 2 cm long.   _____

Test Prep

13. Which is the most appropriate measure for the length of a
    skateboard?

    A. 5 mm   **B.** 5 cm   **C.** 5 dm   **D.** 5 m

14. **Writing in Math** Explain how to give the measurement in
    centimeters of a 56 mm object.

    _____

    _____

Capacity and Metric Units

Choose the most appropriate unit to measure the capacity of each. Write L or mL.

1. water in a bathtub   **2.** perfume in a bottle   **3.** soup in a can

_____   _____   _____

4. Number Sense Which will be less, the number of
liters or the number of milliliters, of the water in a pool?   _____

5. Name something you might measure in liters.

_____

6. Name something you might measure in milliliters.

_____

7. A gallon of milk is the same as 3.78 L of milk.
How many liters of milk are there in 2 gal?   _____

8. A small can of tomato juice contains 56.8 mL of
juice. A large can of tomato juice contains
202.62 mL of juice. How much juice is there in the
large and small can combined?   _____

Test Prep

9. Which capacity would you be most likely to measure in milliliters?

    A. Gas in a car   **B.** Water in a dam

    C. Tea in a cup   **D.** Detergent in a bottle

10. Writing in Math Would you be more likely to measure the
amount of water in your kitchen sink in liters or milliliters? Explain.

_____

_____

Name_____

Mass and Metric Units

Choose the most appropriate unit to measure the mass of each.
Write g or kg.

1. Banana _____   2. Tractor _____   3. Coin _____

4. Bowling ball _____   5. Letter _____   6. Encyclopedia _____

7. **Number Sense** Which is a greater number, the mass of a
cat in grams or the mass of the same cat in kilograms?

_____

8. The *Dromornis stirtoni* was the largest bird
ever. It is now extinct. The ostrich is the
largest living bird. What is the difference
in mass between the *Dromornis stirtoni*
and the ostrich?

Bird	Mass
Ostrich	156 kg
Andean condor	9 kg
Eurasian eagle owl	4.2 kg
Dromornis stirtoni	454 kg

_____

9. Which has a larger mass, an Andean condor or a Eurasian
eagle owl?

_____

10. **Reasoning** A decigram is related to a gram in the same
way a decimeter is related to a meter. How many
decigrams are there in a gram?   _____

Test Prep

11. Which object would be most likely to have a mass of 2 kg?

    A. A truck   **B.** An orange   **C.** A mosquito   **D.** A math book

12. **Writing in Math** Would you be more likely to find the mass
of a pen in grams or in kilograms? Explain.

_____

_____

Name_____

Changing Units and Comparing Measures

Find each missing number.

1. 4,000 mL = _____ L   2. 51 kg = _____ g

3. 7,000 dm = _____ m   4. 600 cm = _____ m

Compare. Write > or < for each $\bigcirc$.

5. 70 g $\bigcirc$ 7 kg   6. 890 cm $\bigcirc$ 9 dm

7. 6 L $\bigcirc$ 900 mL   8. 98 mm $\bigcirc$ 9 cm 9 mm

	Great Gray Owl	Elf Owl	Great Horned Owl
Length	84 cm	160 mm	63 cm
Wingspan	152 cm	380 mm	152 cm
Mass	1.45 kg	4 g	1,800 g

9. Write the owls in order from the least to the greatest mass.

_____

10. How many centimeters long is the elf owl?   _____

Test Prep

11. How many milliliters are there in 32 L?

    A. 32,000   B. 3,200   C. 320   D. 32

12. **Writing in Math** The bird with the longest beak is the
    Australian pelican. The pelican's beak is up to 47 cm long.
    Explain how to find the number of millimeters long the beak is.

_____

_____

Name_____

Writing to Explain

Write to explain.

1. Explain the relationship between a liter and a milliliter.

   _____

   _____

2. Explain how to find the perimeter of
   the rectangle in two different ways.

   _____

   _____

   _____

   _____

3. Explain how the number of shaded
   triangles needed in the design
   compares to the number of
   triangles not shaded.

   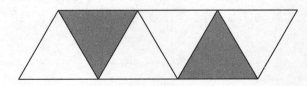

   _____

   _____

4. Explain how to take three different metric measurements of
   a can of fruit cocktail.

   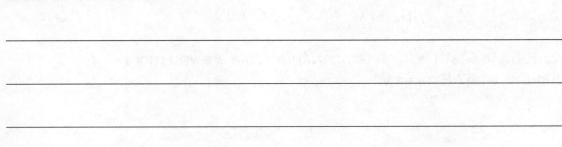

   _____

   _____

   _____

Name _____

Temperature

Read each thermometer. Write the temperature in °C and in °F.

1.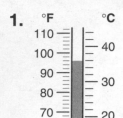

_____

2.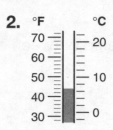

_____

3.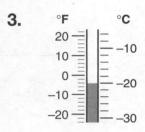

_____

4.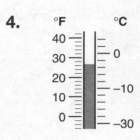

_____

5. **Number Sense** Name one activity you are likely to do outdoors if the temperature is 15°F.

_____

_____

6. A storm front went through and the temperature dropped 10°C in 3 hr. If the temperature started at 6°C, what was the temperature after the 3 hr? _____

Test Prep

7. Which temperature would be best for a day at the beach?

   A. 110°F   **B.** 60°C   **C.** 60°F   **D.** 32°C

8. **Writing in Math** Which temperature scale are you more familiar with? Explain why.

_____

_____

_____

Name_____

Take Out Dinner

Lynn bought a container of Chinese food and brought it home
to eat. The container the rice came in was a cardboard folded
box with a metal handle. Its measurements were 8 cm deep,
10 cm wide, and 12 cm tall.

1. What is the volume of the box the rice came in?   _____

2. Is the container more likely to hold 20 g of rice or 20 kg of
   rice? Explain.

   _____

   _____

   _____

3. With her meal, Lynn got a plastic packet of soy sauce.
   Would you expect the packet to have 20 mL of soy sauce
   or 1 L of soy sauce in it? Explain.

   _____

   _____

4. Lynn also ordered an extra large iced tea. The
   iced tea fills a 2 L container. How many milliliters
   of tea will the container hold?   _____

5. Ruth had $10.54 and paid $2.75 to Taylor for a
   notebook. At a garage sale, Ruth sold a stuffed
   fish for $5.50 and a plastic panda bank for $0.75.
   How much money does Ruth have now?   _____

6. Blocks are used to build a pyramid in the
   pattern shown. How many blocks are needed
   to build a pyramid that has 7 layers?

   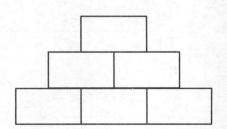

   _____

Inequalities on a Number Line

Name three solutions to each inequality and graph all the
solutions on a number line.

1. $b < 8$ _____

2. $y > 15$ _____

3. $n > 5$ _____

4. $c < 10$ _____

5. A weatherman said the high temperature today will be
above 90°F. Name three temperatures that could be the
high temperature if the weatherman is correct.

_____

6. A ride at the fair says that riders must weigh less than
120 lb. Use the inequality $c < 120$ to find three weights
of people that could go on the ride.

_____

Test Prep

7. Which is a solution to the inequality $x < 16$?

A. 15   **B.** 16   **C.** 17   **D.** 18

8. Writing in Math Is 15.6 a solution to the inequality $b < 15$?
Explain why or why not.

_____

_____

_____

Translating Words to Equations

Write an equation for each sentence.

1. g minus 6 leaves 4. _____

2. 5 times $t = 40$. _____

3. d divided by 7 is 4. _____

4. r less than 16 is 12. _____

5. 7 cars plus f cars equal 21 cars. _____

6. 22 birds less than h birds is 50 birds. _____

Write an equation for each problem.

7. The life span of a swan is up to 50 years in captivity. In the wild, a swan lives up to 19 years. How much longer can a swan live in captivity than in the wild? _____

8. In a conference room, seats are arranged with 6 people around each table. There is seating for 96 in a conference room. How many tables are in the room? _____

Test Prep

9. Which equation matches the sentence?

12 more than y is 19.

A. $12y = 19$ **B.** $\frac{y}{12} = 19$ **C.** $y - 12 = 19$ **D.** $y + 12 = 19$

10. **Writing in Math** Gary has a rope that is 9 ft long. He wants to find out how many inches long the rope is. He uses the equation $\frac{x}{12} = 9$. Will Gary's equation find the correct answer? Explain.

_____

_____

_____

Name_____

Equations and Graphs

Use the equation $y = 2x + 4$. Find the value of y for each value of x.

1. $x = 3$ _____

2. $x = 1$ _____

3. $x = 10$ _____

4. $x = 25$ _____

5. $x = 0$ _____

6. $x = 7$ _____

Graph each equation on the given coordinate graph.

7. $y = 2x$

8. $y = x - 3$

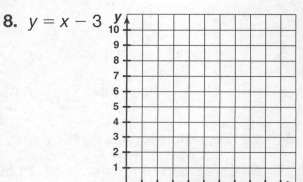

9. Find five ordered pairs on the graph of the equation $y = 3x - 1$.

_____

Test Prep

10. Which equation has the ordered pair (3, 5) as a solution?

A. $y = 2x$ **B.** $y = 2x + 1$ **C.** $y = 2x - 1$ **D.** $y = 3x - 5$

11. Writing in Math Laura looked at the ordered pairs (1, 2), (2, 3), and (3, 4) and said that $1 \times 2 = 2$, so the rule must be $y = 2x$. Is she correct? Explain.

_____

_____

_____

_____

Name_____

Extra or Missing Information

Decide if each problem has extra information or not enough information. Tell any information that is not needed or that is missing. Solve the problem if you have enough information.

1. Angie wrote 5 letters and 7 e-mails on Monday. On Tuesday, she sent the same number of e-mails as she did on Monday, but she wrote 2 fewer letters. On Wednesday, she wrote 4 letters and did not send any e-mails. How many letters did Angie write from Monday through Wednesday?

_____

_____

2. Darrell has 4 boxes of screws that he uses for building wooden toy cars. Each box weighs 10 kg. The cars weigh 200 kg when they are finished. How many screws does Darrell have altogether?

_____

_____

3. Nigel and Cynthia went to the movies. They each had a large drink and they shared a large popcorn. How much did they spend altogether, including their admission?

MOVIES!		
Admission:		$6.00
Drinks:	Large	$2.00
	Small	$1.25
Popcorn:	Large	$3.00
	Medium	$2.25
	Small	$1.75

_____

4. Jessica went to the theater with $10.00. She wants a popcorn and a drink. The movie is 1 hr 44 min long. If she buys a large drink, what is the largest size popcorn Jessica can purchase?

_____

_____

Understanding Probability

Tell whether it is likely, unlikely, impossible, or certain to get each number when each spinner is spun.

Spinner A

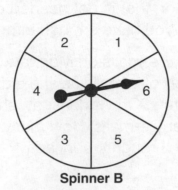
Spinner B

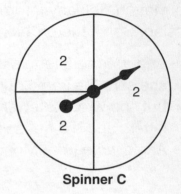
Spinner C

1. 1 on Spinner A _____

2. 2 on Spinner B _____

3. 3 on Spinner A _____

4. 4 on Spinner C _____

5. 2 on Spinner C _____

6. Number Sense A fair game is played in which a player wins if his or her color card is drawn. There are three players and a 30-card deck of red, blue, and green cards. How many red cards are there? _____

Test Prep

7. How many red marbles must there be in a bag of 12 marbles for it to be likely that a red marble is drawn?

A. 4   **B.** 5   **C.** 6   **D.** 7

8. Writing in Math Explain the difference between a fair game and an unfair game.

_____

_____

Listing Outcomes

A coin has two sides, heads and tails. List all the possible outcomes for each situation.

1. Flipping one coin, one time _____

2. Flipping two coins, one time each _____

3. Flipping three coins, one time each

_____

4. **Reasoning** A number cube with the numbers 1, 2, 3, 4, 5, and 6 is tossed two times. Is it likely, unlikely, certain, or impossible for the same number to be tossed both times? _____

5. A deli offers lunch sandwiches for $1.00 with a choice of two cheeses and three meats. How many possible sandwich combinations of one meat and one cheese are there?

_____

Test Prep

6. A coin is flipped twice. Which is the probability that both will be heads?

   A. Likely   **B.** Unlikely   **C.** Impossible   **D.** Certain

7. **Writing in Math** If a coin is flipped, and the spinner is spun, how many total possible outcomes are there? Explain.

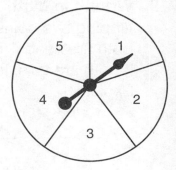

_____

_____

_____

_____

Finding Probability

Write the probability of drawing each letter out of a bag containing the letters in the word MISSISSIPPI.

1. M _____ **2.** I _____ **3.** S _____ **4.** P _____

5. Number Sense If there are 12 possible outcomes, what is the lowest probability that will still make an outcome likely? _____

There are 52 color cards. 13 are red, 13 are blue, 13 are yellow, and 13 are green. Each color has cards numbered from 0 to 12.

6. What is the probability of a card being drawn at random that is red? _____

7. What is the probability of a card being drawn at random that is a 12? _____

Test Prep

8. If the letter tiles are randomly selected, which is the probability of selecting A?

A. $\frac{3}{10}$ **B.** $\frac{2}{10}$

C. $\frac{3}{20}$ **D.** $\frac{1}{10}$

9. Writing in Math A game is played by flipping two coins. One player wins if both are heads. The other player wins if both are tails. Is this a fair game? Explain.

_____

_____

_____

_____

Making Predictions

Use the number tiles for 1–6. Predict how many times you would pick each number. You put the number back after each pick.

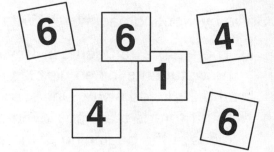

1. 6 when you pick a number 50 times

   _____

2. 1 when you pick a number 12 times

   _____

3. 4 when you pick a number 30 times   _____

4. 5 when you pick a number 10 times   _____

5. An even number when you pick a
   number 60 times   _____

6. An odd number when you pick a number
   36 times   _____

Test Prep

7. When three coins are tossed, how many times out of 100 would you expect the result to be either three heads or three tails?

   A. 10   **B.** 20   **C.** 25   **D.** 30

8. **Writing in Math** Jennifer used a three-color spinner 100 times. Her results are shown. Do you think the spinner was fair? Explain.

Red	Green	Blue
30	29	41

   _____

   _____

   _____

   _____

PROBLEM-SOLVING STRATEGY

Work Backward

Solve by working backward. Write the answer in a complete sentence.

1. There are 21 students in Travis's fourth-grade class. Four new students joined his class after school began this year, and 2 moved away. One student was transferred to another fourth-grade teacher. How many students were in Travis's class at the beginning of the school year?

_____

_____

_____

2. Sir John Franklin was an explorer who traveled in Canada and the United States. He was 33 years old when he began exploring northwestern Canada. In a second expedition 17 years later, he explored as far as Alaska. 11 years later, Franklin died in an expedition in search of a Northwest Passage in 1847. In what year was Franklin born?

_____

3. Tessie has a volleyball game at 7:00 P.M. She needs to be there 20 min early to warm up for the game, and it takes her 45 min to get to the gym. What time should she leave her house?

_____

4. Frank bought lunch for $5.60 at a diner. He spent $2.00 to ride the bus to the mall and back, and spent $6.50 while he was at the mall. His friend Bill paid him back $5.00 that he had borrowed last week. If Frank arrived at home with $10.50 in his pocket, how much did he have when he left home that morning?

_____

PROBLEM-SOLVING APPLICATION   **P 12-10**
Duck Pond Game

Solve. Write the answer in a complete sentence.

In the duck pond game, players draw plastic ducks out of the pond to win a prize. Every player wins a prize. If you draw out a duck with a red mark on the bottom, you win a small prize. If you draw out a duck with a black mark, you win a large prize. If you draw out a duck with a green star, you win an extra large prize. There are 60 ducks in the pond. Two of them have green stars, 6 have black marks, and the rest have red marks.

1. What is the probability of drawing a duck with a red mark?

_____

_____

2. Is it likely, unlikely, impossible, or certain that you will win a prize when you draw out a duck?

_____

3. Each time a duck is drawn, it is returned to the duck pond. Out of 300 draws, how many do you predict will have green stars?

_____

_____

4. As soon as Jack finished dinner last night he spent 2 hr working on his science report, then another 30 min studying for a math test, and 45 min reading a mystery book before he fell asleep. If Jack fell asleep at 10:30 P.M., what time did he finish his dinner?

_____

5. Write an equation for the sentence. Nine years more than Tina's age is 27. Solve the equation for Tina's age.

_____